Community v. Crime

also published by the Bedford Square Press:

Alternative Rural Services: a community initiatives manual
Going Local: neighbourhood social services (NCVO Occasional Paper 1)
Making Work: some examples of Job Creation schemes
Public Participation in Britain: a classified bibliography
Tribunal Representation: the role of advice and advocacy services
Voluntary Organisations: an NCVO directory (1982 edition)
Voluntary and Statutory Collaboration: rhetoric or reality?

COMMUNITY VERSUS CRIME

Colin Moore and John Brown

BEDFORD SQUARE PRESS | NCVO

First published 1981 by the
BEDFORD SQUARE PRESS of the
National Council for Voluntary Organisations
26 Bedford Square London WC1B 3HU

ISBN 0 7199 1059 5 (hardback)
ISBN 0 7199 1060 9 (paperback)

Printed in England by H. Ling Ltd, The Dorset Press,
Dorchester, Dorset

Contents

Preface

This book offers a descriptive analysis of the ways in which information on local crime was gathered, plotted, disseminated, and used as a catalyst for activating police, other statutory agencies, voluntary organisations and communities to work together more effectively to control local crime, and to develop communal strategies in this sphere.

The work presented here is that of the Crime Prevention Support Unit of the Devon and Cornwall Constabulary, set up by the Chief Constable, John Alderson, under the leadership of Colin Moore. From very amateur beginnings, the CPSU taught itself from experience how best – and sometimes how not – to proceed in its work in relation to local circumstances and needs. An analysis of its development was later undertaken by Colin Moore as an M.Sc. thesis in the Department of Social Policy at Cranfield Institute of Technology, under the direction of John Brown. In the course of his research Mr Moore had to re-think many of the assumptions based on seventeen years' experience as an operational detective, causing him to question the whole strategy of present-day policing in England.

That thesis is now re-cast and presented for publication in the belief that the modes of policy and practice it sets out will not only have value in themselves, but may act as a 'Do it Yourself' guide for organisations and communities in other areas who perceive the need – as many increasingly do – to develop communal strategy for crime control.

The authors wish to acknowledge the far-sighted policies of the Devon and Cornwall Police Authority, and of the Chief Constable John Alderson, which made this study possible.

Colin Moore
John Brown

Foreword

Rt. Hon. S. C. Silkin, QC, MP
(Her Majesty's Attorney-General 1974–1979)

The origins of policing lay in the need for local communities to protect themselves from the effects of violence, theft and other offences against their members' interests. They first achieved their aim through the voluntary co-operation of their members.

As society has become more complex and sophisticated, so has policing become more and more a specialist section of society's reactive organisation against breaches of law and order. It fits neatly into the pattern of commission of offence by the criminal, detection and arrest by the police, prosecution by the prosecuting authorities, sentence by the court, detention by the prison authorities. As the pattern has developed, so the police and policing have become more remote from the local community, even in some areas seen as hostile to it; so also have they become divorced from, sometimes inimical to and viewed with suspicion by, the agencies concerned with those weaknesses in society's structure upon which crime feeds.

In recent years there has been a reaction to this development. Nowhere has the reaction been more striking than in Devon and Cornwall, where the Chief Constable has crusaded in support of his twin theses: first that the policeman must reassume his place within the community which he serves; and secondly, but at least as important, that his function is not solely that of reaction to crime, but of 'pro-action', of participation in providing society's preventive medicine.

This interesting and well-documented description of the Devon and Cornwall experiment, known as the Crime Prevention Support Unit, has all the authenticity, crusading spirit and persuasiveness of a work compiled by the Unit's leader, Chief Superintendent Colin Moore, in association with a distinguished academic in the field of social policy, Mr John Brown. It shows how the Unit was established in the City of Exeter, how it took the lead in inserting itself into local 'risk' communities and in bringing together both the members of those communities and the social agencies which served them in order to pool knowledge and ideas and so enable them to be translated into constructive action for the prevention of law-breaking.

How successful has it been? In terms of filling an obvious, and probably widening, gap in society's defences, clearly it has been effective; in terms of crime statistics or of evidence that society has been effectually strengthened and improved, this book does not seek to present evidence or conclusions; these we must await. To the question, why should the police take the lead, it provides the simple answer that no other agency had done so or seemed likely to do so. In other areas there may be room for other methods and other leaders. But at least the book demonstrates that where the police take the lead in co-operation for crime prevention, and do so with the vigour, initiative and enthusiasm inspired by Mr Moore and his Chief Constable, that inspiration can be communicated to others, barriers can be demolished and those who may have come to think of the police as being 'on the other side' can come to appreciate that there is only one side; and that all who seek to make our complex society work more smoothly and harmoniously are on that side.

This book is a most valuable contribution to the debate on the future of policing, which is certain to intensify with the Scarman Report on the Brixton troubles and with the growing signs of adolescent mob violence in target areas in which the police inevitably find themselves to be the target.

July 1981   Sam Silkin

1. Background to the Creation of the Crime Prevention Support Unit

In recent years the apparent increase of lawlessness in our society and the consequent publicity have caused people to question the stability and safety of their communities. Their answers to this threat have mainly been to suggest one or more of the following solutions.

1. Courts should inflict harsher punishments. This is based on the belief that these deter potential offenders. Undoubtedly they do deter some, but can we afford more solutions of this kind? Already the prison population stands at over 43,000; and each male adult prisoner costs over £120 per week, apart from the costs of family dependants who may have to live on the State. Even more startling are the costs of the care and custody of a young person: anything from £5,000 – £12,000 per year.

2. The police should have wider legal powers. This solution fails to take into account Durkheim's warning that a society which would wholly repress crime, would in the process repress all initiative, all non-conformity, all adaptation to change. Fear of apprehension and ensuing prosecution are deterrents to criminal behaviour, but if these can only be achieved by additional encroachments upon our civil liberties, are they worth the cost? There may also be other side effects here, as Wilkins (1) points out:

> if crime and criminals are pursued with too much enthusiasm by law enforcement agencies then the law-abiding citizen may end up changing his fear of crime for a fear of the police – not a very desirable trade-off.

3. Society should become more conscious of security, with wider use of physical means such as locks, bolts and bars. Wheeler (2), for example, comments:

One attraction of physical crime prevention is that it may prove considerably cheaper than attempts to alter attitudes and abilities of potential offenders.

Yet the end of the line here is the concept of a crime-free society only achieved by people living in anti-intruder enclaves such as are now being built in the United States of America, where people live rather as they did in the early West in their forts, but now surrounded by surveillance devices, dogs and private security armies. Is this really acceptable or economic?

4. Increase police numbers. This is a favourite police solution, though since 1966 we have seen police numbers rise from 86,000 to over 110,000, whilst crime has escalated. And can society afford a much bigger, and better paid, Police Force?

All these 'solutions' have been researched and tested: and the best that can be said of any of them is that their effectiveness is questionable.

For their part, the police have pursued, or have been required to pursue, a number of policies aiming to improve their effectiveness. There have been amalgamations of police forces, so that their numbers have dwindled from hundreds to just over forty in a period of a few years. Large investments have been made at national and local levels to provide communication networks, computers, cars, radio and other sophisticated equipment. Pressures to achieve maximum use of resources have also led to centralisation of manpower, resulting in fewer policemen walking their beat and more and more diverted to newly created specialist squads – Drugs, Regional Crime Squads, Crime Prevention Units, Defensive Weapons and so on.

Because of their specialised training and limited objectives, the squads have responded to their tasks in highly organised ways, and invariably the measures of successes claimed by these units have been based on quantitative modes of measurement, e.g. numbers of people arrested, numbers of stops and searches in the street, numbers of search warrants executed, numbers of offences detected, etc. In brief, the whole emphasis has been upon *quantity* rather than upon *quality* of police work.

In its search for efficiency, the police service has rarely considered those qualitative modes of assessment which are so often used by citizens and by other agencies to judge police success. The claim by the old lady that the neighbourhood is quieter since the children have become involved in a police recreational scheme, is a qualitative perception which in real terms is just as, or more, important than the quantitative fact that no crimes were reported.

But what does the public expect or want from the police? I have been unable to find any research which gives me answers. In an effort to gain some knowledge, I have, at times, in talks around the Devon and Cornwall area, invited public audiences to define the criteria on which they judge the success of the police. Although this is not in any way a reliable indicator, there is sufficient repetition to indicate that it is the qualitative approach that is used by the citizen, e.g.:

Camborne: Sincerity, helpfulness, understanding ability, deterrent effect, approachability.

Plymouth: Social ability, responsibility, dignity, sincerity, approachability, simplicity, impartiality, co-operation, detection of serious crime, crime prevention, trustworthy, understanding, sympathy.

Exmouth: Friendliness, helpfulness, co-operation, understanding, prevention, responsibility.

Exeter: Trust, unity (public/police partnership), understanding, helpfulness, mutual co-operation. Time spent in listening, caring attitude, contact, public relations, problem solving.

This demonstrates that community conceptions of the police role are often fundamentally different from those held by policemen. It also emphasises a need to revalue policing methods to ensure that we try to serve the ends that communities desire. If we fail to do so, we are certainly in danger of forfeiting their support and co-operation.

In 1977 the Home Office Crime Policy Planning Organisation issued a paper entitled. *A Review of the Criminal Justice Policy 1976* (3), commenting that:

In view of the limitations in the capacity of the agencies of the Criminal Justice system to reduce the incidence of crime, the scope for reducing crime through policy that goes beyond the boundaries of the Criminal Justice system merits particular attention. . . . any changes in attitude amongst delinquents are likely to derive from changes in social policy and public attitudes rather than from activity within the Criminal Justice system.

This is a tacit acknowledgement of the increasing ineffectiveness of the criminal justice system, including the police. (A similar claim was made about the control of disease in the 1980 Reith Lectures by Professor Ian Kennedy, when he argued that it was not the medical profession that caused such plagues as cholera, TB or diphtheria to disappear, but improvements in such factors as housing, nutrition and sanitation.)

This Home Office view is supported by my own research which has found within a city, even within a neighbourhood, significantly distinctive patterns of crime and delinquency. It would seem that these are often influenced by social policies implemented by housing managers, planners, transport authorities and other statutory agencies. Environmental factors such as transport, lighting, and access to commercial amenities such as pubs and night clubs, also play their part in the formation of these patterns. These patterns also raise questions about the comparative weaknesses and strengths of informal control systems in specific neighbourhoods.

These positive sources and forces for self-regulation need to be identified and supported if we are to control crime, since they constitute the essential *resources* in this sphere, police resources themselves being merely peripheral to crime control. Recognition of this fact provides the basis for planning strategies to combat crime.

Newman (4), in his opening paragraphs of *Defensible Space*, rightly emphasises that crime problems will not be answered through increased manpower. He blames the breakdown of the social mechanisms that once kept crime in check on the virtual disappearance of small-town environments, both rural and urban, which once framed and enforced their moral codes.

Newman emphasises that in our modern society there are very few instances of shared beliefs or values among physical neighbours, and although this heterogeneity may be intellectually desirable, it has crippled our ability to agree on the action required to maintain a cohesive social framework:

> It is clear to almost all researchers in crime prevention that the issue hinges on the instability of communities to come together in joint action. The physical environment we have been building in our cities for the past twenty-five years, actually prevents such amity and discourages the natural pursuit of collective action. The anonymous cities we have built for maximum freedom and multiple choice may have inadvertently succeeded in severely curtailing many of our previous options. Collective community action, once easy, is now cumbersome. But even in the absence of community of minds, joint action has become essential to the survival of urban life in America. Police forces operating without community consent, direction and control, are a wasted effort, more irritant than deterrent. Means must be found for bringing neighbours together, if only for the limited purpose of ensuring survival of their collective milieu.

Newman places much of the blame on the nature of the physical environment created in recent years. However, other changes in our society have been equally or even more devastating in weakening or disrupting our community patterns: mass unemployment, particularly amongst the young; racial problems; the decay of our inner cities; industrial strife; civil demonstrations; the weakening influence of the church; the loosening of family structures: these and many others have all contributed to an air of uncertainty in our social structure and values. Social and geographical mobility has also served to weaken relationships and local control systems; and a society which is changing in these ways has fewer accepted standards of social conduct than a closely integrated society.

What are the factors that keep the great majority of citizens law-abiding most of the time? Jacobs (5) emphasises that:

> The public peace, the sidewalks and street peace of cities is not kept primarily by the police, necessary as police are. It is kept primarily by

an intricate almost unconscious network of voluntary controls and standards among the people themselves, and enforced by the people themselves. No amount of police can enforce civilisation where the normal, casual enforcement of it has broken down.

What is this 'intricate almost unconscious network of voluntary controls and standards'? Banton (6) argues that social compliance derives primarily from the informal controls built up into everyday relations. Preservation of the peace requires a certain public acceptance of the social order, agreement about norms regulating personal relations, and a recognition at other times that it is unprofitable to challenge rules and regulations backed by a superior force. In everyday affairs, compliance with most rules does not depend upon the likelihood of them being enforced, but upon an acceptance of informal norms and concern for the feeling of others. This has been more succinctly described by Brown (7):

> The most important Police Force in any society is the capacity of that society to regulate itself. This capacity derives primarily from the strength and quality of the society's family and community life, of its social, economic, political and other institutional structures, and of its cultural traditions and values.

It therefore seems that the best way to keep the peace is to reinforce these informal controls. But this implies a fundamental reappraisal of policing methods so as to create coherent policies which bring preventive and reactive policing into appropriate balance in response to the local circumstances and needs.

There are thus two possible approaches to policing society. The first is our present system where the police are largely *reacting* to ever-increasing demands. This system can be summarised as follows:–

Crime Investigation →Crime Detection →Punishment

This model of policing is clearly incomplete since it denies preventive approaches to policing, though some would argue that certain forms of 'reactive' policing have preventive effects. But can effective preventive approaches to policing be developed which are not based on authoritarian measures? An interesting analogy can be drawn here from an article by the motoring correspondent of *The Times* (8 November 1977), in which the Metropolitan Police Accident Prevention Unit claimed that, as a result of research, they had prevented accidents. This had been accomplished in the following ways:

(a) An examination of the location of road accidents in London revealed that 70% occurred in the same localities. These localities only represented 17% of the total road network in the Metropolitan Police area.
(b) The traffic flows at these 'black spots' were analysed by scientists who then recommended road improvements, such as improved traffic signals or structural alterations.
(c) An intensive two-week prevention programme based on cautioning and advising drivers at these black spots was carried out by uniformed policemen.
(d) As a result of these actions, there had been a dramatic improvement in driver behaviour long after the squad had moved on.
(e) A year's activity had shown a *reduction* of nearly 25% in road accidents at these locations.

If the police carried out similar research into the problems of crime and delinquency, analysing the location of crime and offenders and taking remedial action which did not involve authoritarian measures, then arguably this could result in the prevention and reduction of crime.

The new model would be:

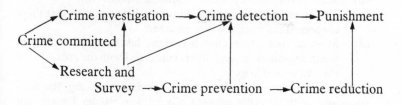

These measures can be taken if the police accept and understand that the real sources for the control of crime and disorder are in the community. If this is acknowledged, then the police must accept responsibility to activate or support such controls. Alderson, in his booklet *Resources to Ideas* (8), calls this activation 'pro-active policing'.

There are precedents for such action in our police history. The first that I can trace was in 1957 when David Gray, then a Chief Constable (later Her Majesty's Chief Inspector of Constabulary for Scotland), initiated integrated social action in an area called Gibshill in Scotland. In a letter to the Town Clerk he wrote:

I have to inform you that the environment in some districts is such that boys growing up in them commit petty crimes and acts of vandalism, not because of inherent badness, but because they are conforming to the pattern of behaviour set by many of those around them who show little respect for property or for law and order.

It goes without saying that if money was available and social, police and other services could be increased, then improvements would follow. Such a position is unlikely to arise for a very long time . . . but I do feel that in certain areas money spent on improving amenities, can be money wasted, unless effort is made by the police and others to protect and maintain what is provided.

The aim would be *to select an area* and concentrate the attention of the police, the local authority services, the churches, teachers, and others, to produce a better environment for children to play and grow up in.

If the corporation decide to take action, planning on the following lines would probably be necessary:-

(a)   Initial discussion and preparation of a plan by members of corporation.

(b)   Survey area and list possible improvements and cost.

(c)   Decide on improvements and prepare time tables so that those concerned can work and plan together.

(d)   Meet in conference church leaders, headmasters, leaders of youth organisations, and others concerned with the area. Obtain their views and help.

If this experiment is attempted, I envisage policing the area rigorously, with specially selected officers who would, I hope, not only protect the property and enforce the law, but attempt to gain the confidence and respect of the majority of the people in the area, and particularly of the children. The officers selected would of necessity require to show an interest in matters outside the scope of ordinary police work and constant effort would be needed to maintain close liaison between them and parents, churches and schools serving the district.

Later, in 1974, James Haughton, then Chief Constable of Liverpool, initiated a similar scheme in Kirkby. Both schemes concerned geographical areas characterised by alienation and multiple systems of disaffection, ranging from criminality to physical dereliction. The Gibshill project is still in being and has, over the years, produced improvement to the quality of life of the people. Implicit in both these projects was the concept of the essential interdependence of statutory and voluntary social agencies in the task of social crime prevention. I believe that these two case studies are classics of what police leadership can achieve in pro-active policing.

I should make it clear that I am not arguing against reactive policing. It is an essential part of police duty which must be continually improved. What I am suggesting is that pro-active policing can assist the reactive role by reducing the total numbers of crimes that need investigation. More importantly, it will ensure continued public support and co-operation. This again assists our reactive role.

How is this to be accomplished?

Speaking at a Police Federation seminar at Cambridge in 1976, John Alderson, Chief Constable of Devon and Cornwall, emphasised the tradition of citizen and community responsibility for crime control. He thought this to be in danger and warned that a shift away from it could involve the expense of bigger police forces and the danger of quasi-military police with law enforcement as practised in totalitarian states. Already there were signs of the modern Police Force concentrating more and more of its resources into the investigation of crime, its detection and prosecution, and into developing its techniques of reaction by the use of technology. But in this pursuit, he argued, the police had neglected to develop a broad based crime prevention policy, relying on the fact that fear of detection is in itself a deterrent. He went on to advocate that the police should develop a new concept of preventing crime by activating the community to its responsibilities (12):

> I suggest contemporary problems of crime demand greater resources for its combatting than our present economy can afford. To combat crime the Police and the citizen have to get down to this business together. Thus police instead of feeling they are alone should take steps to convert the ample sympathy for their cause into active support. Equally the citizen can no longer say, 'I have paid for a Police Force to do this job, it is therefore no longer my responsibility.'

This was Alderson's central concept for preventing crime by pro-active policing, i.e. motivating the good in society. He ended his speech by emphasising that the police alone cannot contain the rise of crime even if society provides them with additional resources.

He put this concept into action by forming the Crime Prevention Support Unit (CPSU) with the following terms of reference:

1. To examine facts and statistics in selected police areas with a view to the identification of crime and community problems.
2. To produce and experiment with new ideas in crime prevention initiatives.
3. To encourage and direct available police resources to the prevention of crime.
4. To harness available public support including the unemployed in activities to teach good citizenship and thereby prevent crime.

Initially the Unit consisted of six policemen, but within months it was reduced to five, then four, and was led for three years by the writer of this book.

The original area chosen for the experiment was the city of Exeter, in many ways ideal for testing the efficacy of preventive policing. First, it was a well balanced community of 100,000 with District Council status, and could be described as a microcosm of larger cities. Since 1945 a large part of the city centre had been rebuilt. The inner city area was rapidly changing from being inhabited by families in large terraced houses to multiple bed-sits. This transformation had come about because of the growth of the local university and English Language schools, and the consequential need to house students, both English and foreign. On the outskirts of the city there had been built large private and council-owned housing estates, producing a variety of social and delinquency problems.

Second, and more importantly, in 1976 there had been changes in policing methods. During the eighty years of this century Exeter has experienced three distinct forms of policing:

1. In the first twenty-five years the city had been divided into small geographical sectors in which the same sergeants and constables worked a rota system.
2. The introduction of the police telephone box system throughout the city in the 1920s saw a change, with an emphasis on the sergeants and their teams rotating all about the city.
3. The 1960s saw the introduction of the Panda Car system, the building of a new central Police Headquarters and the growth of specialised Police Departments, all of which led to a centralisation of police resources.

The second and third changes in policing methods came about as a result of new technology, on the premise that this would lead to an improved service, in particular in speed of response to emergencies, though others have argued it has led to a deterioration in service. However, there is no doubt that these changes, particularly those in the 1960s, led to impaired continuity in the policing of the same geographical areas. The public have complained about 'anonymous' policemen and about delays or failures to deal with their more mundane everyday complaints, such as cars parking on footpaths, and policemen have complained about frequent changes in their duties and beats: all pointing to a gradual decline in effectiveness, made manifest by more and more complaints about police from the public.

Eventually, in 1975, the Police Chief Superintendent in charge of Exeter set up a working party under the chairmanship of his deputy to examine the policing system and to make recommendations. His deputy had a great deal of experience of rural policing, was determined to set up a similar system in the city, and within a few months the working party recommended and introduced a system which decentralised uniform patrol officers. The city was split into five sections, and in four of them a sergeant and twelve constables were given the task and responsibility for policing *their own area*. The fifth area was the city centre, which had a larger proportion of policemen, and continued to accept responsibility for the 24-hour emergency response throughout the city. Each section had a number of resident constables (later called community constables) who each had his own beat and was able to choose his own hours of work. These and other changes in the Divisional Police Headquarters led to an overall increase both in efficiency and morale. Furthermore, it was obvious from public remarks that they welcomed back the 'walking bobby'. Many cynics said that Exeter Police had done nothing more than to 'rediscover the wheel', but as a result of the CPSU projects which were carried out in 1976/1977 the functions of these 'bobbies' were even further extended.

The projects undertaken by the CPSU are described and analysed in the following chapters, together with the reactions to them by police, by practitioners in other agencies and by people in local communities. Appendix A defines the methods by which the projects were researched.

2. Methods of Analysing Local Crime Problems

The first crucial step of the Crime Prevention Support Unit was to develop effective methods of analysing crime and community problems. This was necessary because the police statistical tables told us almost nothing on this score. It was therefore decided to try to bring together police and other relevant information in ways that would be generally understandable to other agencies and to the community. It was hoped that this would enhance both its authenticity and its acceptability.

The objectives of that analysis were:

1. To identify what crime is committed, when and where; and also what crime is committed by juveniles.
2. To plot area distributions of crime against general characteristics of, and facilities in, those areas.
3. To identify the areas where juveniles are most at risk, and to plot these against general characteristics of the areas.
4. To provide this information to generalist and specialist Police Units in the area; to other service and statutory agencies; and to community and other voluntary groups.
5. To use this information supply to stimulate police thinking about the appropriate balance between reactive and pro-active policing in response to local circumstances and needs.
6. To use this information supply to alert those responsible for local services on matters relating to crime and the environment; to engender a sense of common concern amongst social agencies and local communities; and thus both to stimulate co-operation and coordination among these organisations, and to mobilise community resures for self-regulation.

Spot-mapping is not new to the police service. Most detectives at some time or other have used this technique to study a particular pattern of crime. The 'old' Exeter City Force in the last war had its map room with separate maps displaying specific categories of reported crime. Spot-maps have also been used as a simple diagrammatic summary of facts by researchers such as Booth, Burgess, Thrasher, Zorbaugh and more recently by McClintock, Downs, Baldwin, Morris and many others.

It was decided to use this method to spot-map the location of specific categories of crime for the year 1976. This meant an examination of several thousand crimes in the crime register which was held at the police Headquarters. Because of the enormity of this task, it was decided to be selective in the types of crime that were to be extracted. Members of the unit had already learned in their initial contact with both the citizens and the statutory agency workers, that most concern was expressed about street crimes and burglaries. They are perhaps seen as the most threatening because they are crimes of personal confrontation, and hence most destructive of feelings of safety and security.

The following crimes were therefore chosen:

Crimes of Violence	–	serious assault, other assaults, robbery
Vandalism	–	malicious damage over £20
Joy-riding	–	theft and taking motor vehicles without the consent of the owner
Theft from cars	–	stealing from motor vehicles
Burglaries	–	burglaries of shops, stores, offices, schools, etc; burglaries of dwelling houses.

These reported crimes account for over 40% of Exeter's total annual crime.

A young police constable, Mr Linsdell, observed the maps in the making and suggested that it would be far more interesting if the information was overlaid on to one single map of Exeter. This was done by transferring the information on to view-foils and using an overhead projector. The projected picture showed the statistics in a new perspective. Although the different categories of crime had been colour coded it was immediately noticeable that some areas disappeared under a black morass due to the number of reported crimes clustered in certain streets. These 'black spots', or 'crime priority areas' as they became known,

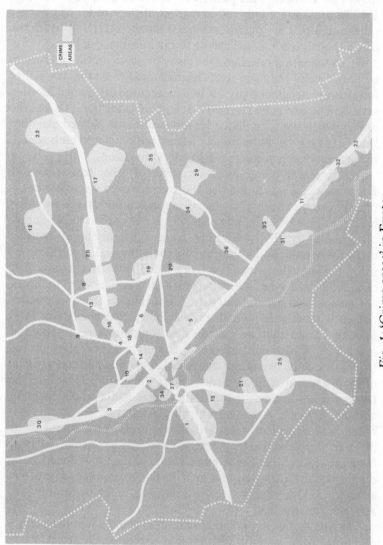

Fig. 1: 'Crime areas' in Exeter

CRIME AREAS

fanned out from the city centre towards the outskirts as the spokes on a wheel. This pattern is reproduced on page 15 (Fig. 1). The areas are numbered in respect of their order of priority, i.e. the area that has the most crime is numbered '1'. (A list of the CPSU's analysed material can be found in Appendix B.)

An examination revealed that many of our crime areas were to be found along the main roads leading away from the city centre towards the peripheral private and local authority owned housing estates. The one main road that seemed to suffer the least was the one in which the City Police Headquarters was located. Another 'trail' of crime could be followed from the city night club area to the nearest concentration of 'take-away' food bars.

As the research continued a number of other facts emerged. For instance, it was found that these crime areas were *constant* in their size and pattern. Only one disappeared during the two-year research. This was a building site which was used as an adventure playground by the youngsters from a neighbouring housing estate. When the builder eventually took physical precautions by using fencing, the criminal activity faded away and disappeared completely when the new owners took up occupancy.

Criminal activity did fluctuate from time to time, of course, but each month the overall predictability rate was about 70%. Specific crimes such as vandalism in some areas represented as much as 85% of their total crime; and certain locations suffered from just one or two crime categories. This was particularly true of those areas around car parks, where the motor car became the target for auto-crime; though other areas had a whole range of criminal activity, ranging from burglaries and assault to auto-crime and vandalism. Obviously some areas were found to be more criminally active than others, especially as one moved away from the city centre; and an examination of the times at which the crimes occurred showed that most of the areas were most active at night. A few were active both day and night, with only two active during the day.

The fact that a car park or road system could affect the pattern of crime made us look deeper into the crime areas. A study showed that many crimes clustered around specific amenities, such as night clubs, certain youth clubs, take-away food bars, pubs and car parks. Newman (1) has also focused attention on this subject. He quotes examples where the proximity of certain types of buildings act to impair the safety of the neighbourhood, and particularly singles out schools and food bars:

> A recurring problem of such a position results from the close proximity of housing projects with High Schools and Junior Colleges. In much the same way where an area of the housing project faces on a teenage hamburger joint or games room hangout, the buildings immediately opposite have higher crime rates. Two hamburger joints on the west side of the project and the teenage play areas on the east generate high crime and vandalism in the immediate adjacent buildings. The New York City Housing Authority Police have found that those of its projects located adjacent to Commercial Street suffered proportionately higher crime rate.

Newman concludes that not all buildings enhance the safety of a street or neighbourhood, and emphasises that each building must be critically evaluated in terms of its business, the times of its use, the type of person using it, and their relationship with local residents.

Jacobs (2) also highlights the problem of licensed premises:

> Nightspots are today overwhelming the streets and the very life of the area. In a district excellent at handling and protecting strangers they have concentrated *too many strangers*. All in too irresponsible a mood for any conceivable city society to handle naturally.

However, our research showed that in some instances these amenities were not present in crime areas. In fact, the more we studied the patterns the more questions were raised in our minds. How did the nature of the environment affect the location of crime? Did the positioning of amenities within the city dictate where crime would occur? Was it the amenity that created the stimuli, or was it the increased criminal opportunity around it? Why was it that some amenities were not in crime areas – was it because they were subject to a greater degree of control, or that they were run by the local community?

Analysis of youth crime proved of particular interest. Over a period of eight years there had been a four-fold increase in the number of young offenders in Devon and Cornwall. (For the purposes of the research, a young offender was defined as a person under the age of seventeen years who was caught by the police and admitted, or was found guilty of, burglary, assault, theft of vehicles, theft or vandalism.) It was decided to spot-map the addresses of the known young offenders in Exeter over a period of three years – 1974, 1975 and 1976. It was hoped by doing this to answer such questions as:

(a) Where did the young offenders live?
(b) What type of crime were they committing?
(c) Do different neighbourhoods have different trends in crime or age groups?

The information was extracted by manually searching three years of indices. Addresses were colour coded according to the crime for which the young person had come to the notice of the police. This identified the streets where the young people were most at risk. By detailed chart analysis one could monitor whether the delinquency in those streets was apparently increasing, constant, or decreasing. Also, one could identify particular trends in the types of crimes and/or the age groups concerned. The tough reputation for delinquency of certain housing estates was seen to be localised in one or two streets, for which the whole locality suffered. 'Black' and 'white' streets were found alongside each other on the same estate. The findings were similar to those found by Jones (3) in his study of Leicester. It demonstrated that the addresses of young offenders were not widely and evenly dispersed throughout the city but were closely localised, often in one or two or three streets of an estate or contiguous group of streets. Sometimes the cluster of spots were apparently confined by some obvious barrier of social intercourse – i.e. railway track, park, main road, the boundary of a housing estate or where the local authority housing estate gave way to one which was privately owned.

A comparative study of the three years demonstrated that certain streets were cause of concern, and these were labelled 'juveniles at risk' areas. A map displaying these designated areas in

known is shown fully in Fig. 1P (Fig. 2). The Riot has attacked
related entire areas to characteristics of local environments and

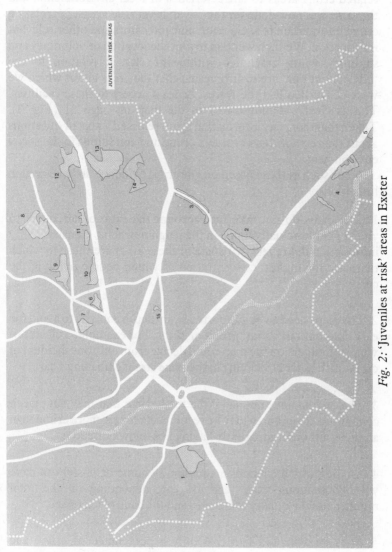

Fig. 2: 'Juveniles at risk' areas in Exeter

available everyone in the police if the police has a similar no
amateur P fraction process developed a discriminating prin-

Exeter is displayed on page 19 (Fig. 2). The unit had already related crime areas to characteristics of local environments, and the same was now done for the 'juveniles at risk' areas, i.e. relating crime information to socio-economic indicators and other relevant information. We then went on to plot the location of voluntary and statutory youth amenities within the city in relation to the 'juveniles at risk' areas. It revealed that the areas about which we were concerned had the fewest or least access to these facilities. This is clearly demonstrated in the map on page 21 (Fig. 3). Taken together, this information again released a host of questions about the relationships between crime and conditions in the social environment.

Maps such as these based on empirical evidence do have certain limitations:

1. The maps do not take into account the ratio of offenders to young people actually living in the neighbourhood. Census (1971) information did reveal that some of these areas are those in which there are the highest concentration of young people living in the city.

2. The maps need to be supported by in-depth analysis to avoid too easy assumptions about 'problem' areas. For example, a cluster of young offenders on the map could derive from only one incident of crime such as six boys living in the same street damaging a car.

3. The coding does not show the total crime that may have been committed. So one area may be responsible for far more crime than another, although apparently having less known offenders.

4. An area which contains a community home or hostel can have wild fluctuations from year to year, depending on the total number and the quality of inmates and the control exercised.

5. It is an accepted fact that only a percentage of crime and criminals ever come to the notice of the police for a variety of reasons. Therefore, we were only displaying the 'official' picture.

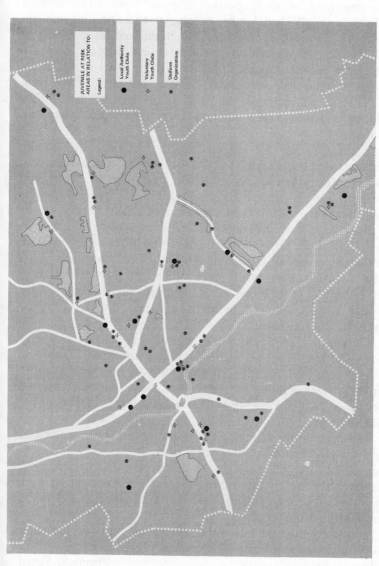

Fig. 3: 'Juveniles at risk' areas in Exeter seen in relation to the provision of statutory and voluntary youth organisations

However, our information represented what McClintock (4) has described as an 'important starting point and continual reference point'. And I must emphasise that the unit was not seeking a multitude of anomie/sub-cultural theories, psychological theories, differential associations or interactionist theories. The purpose was to establish facts sufficient to act as a basis for action by police and community: and a central fact deriving from the analysis was certainly the relationship between local policy making and local crime patterns, over which police have no control.

It was apparent, for instance, that a decision by a Planning Committee to grant permission for someone to open a night club could create a crime area and that a decision by a Housing Committee to recommend lower rents for some of their properties could be the start of a 'juveniles at risk' area in that street.

The next step was to gauge public reactions to our information: First of all councillors, planners, policemen and selected members of the general public were invited to the office to view the maps. The questions they asked were numerous. Because of their responses and subsequent encouragement, visual displays were given to representatives of numerous agencies, to the local council and to the general public.

This was the information that was used to activate people at neighbourhood level through community meetings. They saw their streets displayed; their 'juveniles at risk' area with its youth outlets, or lack of them; and the relevant background information. To this was added a display of information gleaned from door-to-door surveys.

The community meetings that followed can be described as invigorating, traumatic, and exhausting. It was two-way communication. The initial meetings were purely police-oriented, but later we have found it more useful to involve representatives from the other statutory agencies, such as Education, Social Services and Youth and Community.

What were the reactions of the representatives of the agencies, councillors, policemen and community? As our method of diagnosis became known, so these agencies – Planners, Social Services, Probation, Education, Sports Council and others – took an increasing interest in it. Some were suspicious of police motives and questioned us closely as to what use we were going to put it. They were afraid it would be used to create further stigmatisation of certain areas in the city. Some were concerned that it would expose weaknesses in agencies' use of resources. Others expressed the opinion that the information should be kept confidential. Some saw it as raising questions about certain decisions by local politicians. Gradually, however, more and more took an increasing interest in the data.

The Youth and Community Officer with the responsibility for providing and co-ordinating youth and community activities and amenities in Exeter was the first to start using the information. He redeployed some of his resources into the 'juveniles at risk' areas. As he explained, no-one had ever identified the streets to him. More importantly, he implemented a survey amongst the young people in those areas, so that the results could be shared and also used in his long-term planning for the city.

Some myths were exploded which magistrates, social workers and others had about certain housing estates. Others were confirmed. The Planning Officer welcomed the information and used it at a regional planning conference. The Housing Manager was anxious to have sight of the data as constituting a new perspective of his housing estates; and he found it useful both to question policies which he had implemented, and to help him formulate others. Amongst other things it helped him to re-define his definition of a problem family, which until then had been based on failure to pay rent, the number of repairs required for a house and the number of complaints received from neighbours.

Some councillors expressed concern about their own wards. A few saw the results as a reason for demanding more resources, whilst others took positive steps in consulting the unit and other statutory agencies with a view to activating the communities. Their views varied. One commented that crime was a fact of life and that nothing could be done other than controlling it with harsher punishments and more policemen. Another councillor was concerned about revealing the effects of certain amenities on the location of crime. He foresaw difficulties in obtaining planning permission for certain buildings, or for changes in their use. He commented that his first priority was, and would always be, to increase the rate (tax) revenue for the city.

On the basis of its research, the CPSU warned about the effects of large leisure amenities on the location of crime. It was pointed out that a small community-based amenity, whether a pub, local fish and chip shop or voluntary youth club, was far better absorbed by the neighbourhood. Furthermore, if the city really wanted to combat delinquency, then small community based resources must be made available on the vast local authority housing estates. Many councillors, members of the press and the public heard this message and accepted it without a murmur until it became linked to the proposed building of a commercial leisure centre in Exeter. Suddenly the message promulgated by the Unit was seen as threatening to this prestigious project on which one political party had set its heart. A newspaper article used the Unit's data to question the impact that the leisure centre would have on its neighbourhood and delinquency in the city. It concluded that it might have a detrimental effect on the surrounding neighbourhood and would certainly not help combat delinquency.

Because of this publicity the Chief Constable and members of the Unit came under pressure from politicians and officers of the local council to withdraw from this dispute. Although this did not occur, the incident emphasised to policemen the political dimensions of the CPSU's work. We had believed that as the comments were based on empirical research they would be seen as neutral observations – a naive assumption based on a police tradition of seeing themselves as politically neutral. But ironically, this 'political' interference actually enhanced our standing in the eyes of other statutory agency workers who had often expressed concern about the problems of political pressure.

The results of the analysis also provoked a variety of responses from policemen. Some displayed cynical amusement, dismissing the information as useless. Others questioned its truthfulness, criticising the failure to show police successes in detection. Several supervisory policemen expressed concern about revealing the data, seeing it as a personal criticism of their effectiveness. But others began to use the data to brief their men and to deploy resources in the crime areas. Fluctuations in these areas were noticed, and immediately claimed as proof of their management ability. A minority of detectives started to monitor the crime data pictures connecting together specific spates of crime.

The community responses were as mixed and as varied. In one locality they identified certain lawful activities that took place in a crime area which, they suggested, could be attractions or catalysts for unlawful behaviour, e.g. they identified a little known sports club hidden in the depth of an industrial estate. On certain nights of the week it held public 'discos' which attracted large numbers of young people. An examination of the dates of their functions coincided with the timing of the crime area in which it was located. They also questioned why the authorities had allowed certain environmental decisions to be taken such as building a housing complex next to three night clubs and three public houses. They further questioned why there were not more uniformed foot patrols, seeing this as the main deterrent of crime. They wanted more contact with the police and thought foot patrols the best way to re-establish it.

At times there was relief that so few crimes were committed; at others a call for capital and corporal punishment. Every meeting produced strong responses, whether at the time or later. In some cases they led to the creation of a community organisation, or just to a few mothers starting to meet together.

The crime maps were displayed to several thousand Exeter people; to individuals, to small groups, to mass meetings, to representatives of most local statutory agencies, political, cultural and voluntary organisations. During that time only one complaint was received about releasing such information, from a lady who expressed concern that the road adjoining her address was designated a 'juveniles at risk' area. She saw this as undermining her status at her place of employment.

Amongst the variety of responses a number of people pressed for creative action; and Unit members decided to make a number of initiatives designed to activate agencies (including policemen) and the community. These are set out in the next chapter.

3. Activating Communities: Problems and Case Studies

It was argued in Chapter 1 that the control of crime and the security of urban life depend less on the presence of police officers than on the quality and strength of the inhabitants' informal control systems. Neighbourhoods with weakening informal control systems will suffer from increasing levels of crime.

The most researched example is Pruitt-Igoe in St Louis, Missouri. This low-income housing project, which consisted of 43 buildings containing 2,800 flats, was completed in the mid 1950s. It was acclaimed as a 'shining addition to the city's skyline, a new hope for the city's poor' (1). Fifteen years later Pruitt-Igoe was emptied of inhabitants and dynamited. It was deliberately levelled by its housing corporation because everyone agreed that it was a disastrous failure. Instead of developing into a shining example of twentieth-century low-rent housing, the 25 million dollar project had developed into a battle ground between criminal and victim; robberies, rapes and other serious crimes were prevalent. The flats, play areas, open spaces, stairways and elevators were all locations for crime. Instead of being places where people could enjoy themselves they became areas of fear, littered with rubbish, beer cans and excrement. Similar conditions developed in a much smaller housing project, nicknamed the Piggeries, in Liverpool.

Oscar Newman, Yancey (2) and others placed much blame on the architectural errors which turned Pruitt-Igoe into a crime-ridden bad land, reminiscent of the early American West. They thought it wrongly planned, in violation of almost everything known about human requirements. The dark landings and stairways meant that respectable inhabitants locked themselves in their flats afraid to venture out or to socialise with neighbours. But there were other damaging factors which are sometimes over-looked by those who blame the planners. Over half of the people who lived in the housing project existed on Government welfare payments and many were single-parent families (usually without fathers). Unemployment levels were high. Consequently the people who lived there were hardly able to control their environment and had little sense of responsibility towards it. Moore (3) succinctly commented:

> The local housing authority makes most decisions for him (the Pruitt-Igoe resident). He is told the length of time he may have a house guest, the kind of pet he may own (goldfish or birds only), the paint he can put on the walls, the kind of floor covering he may use, and the scheduled day he may sweep his steps and use the laundry room.

Although housed, the residents never felt part of their physical environment and were unable to pursue their goals within an environment of other individuals, groups and organisations. No amount of reactive policing could ever change it as police could not be everywhere. No traditional policing system could ever establish or re-establish an informal control system in Pruitt-Igoe. Therefore, the project never became a community and that failure was total, for few human beings can survive except in community.

A police constable's graphic description of the life style in our Liverpool Piggeries (4) makes similar points:

> This area historically is a deprived area ... There is a lack of communication with outside bodies, there is also a lack of communication amongst the people themselves. You get the situation of an emotionally crippled boy marrying an emotionally crippled girl and what can you expect as a result? Their kids are going to be brought up in exactly the same way as they were and the whole cycle starts again. Until you find some way of breaking that cycle you are going to get nowhere and I can't see any government providing the necessary funds to change this situation. It's not political enough, it's always been here, it just gets a little bit worse each year. It doesn't attract sufficient attention and no government is going to go out on a limb to finance or fund the necessary schools or closed centres which are required for the short term ... But I do feel very strongly that the cycle has got to be broken somehow because otherwise we are just playing around.

Although disasters on the scale of Pruitt-Igoe and the Piggeries are relatively few, many people will be quick to identify similar currents of alienation in our vast local authority housing estates or

in some ethnic ghettoes. These man-made disaster areas emphasise the dual nature of the concept of community. On one level it
means a group of persons living in a specific location subject to
some form of bureaucratic control. On another level it also means a
sense of fraternity or solidarity which is an indispensable com-
ponent of every successful community. Ralph Linton (5) argued
that every human has the need for companionship, reassurance
and·emotional security which comes from belonging to a social
unit whose members share similar ideas and patterns of behaviour.
Any person requires from those around (whether family, friends
or fellow workers) co-operation so as to be provided with
food, work and security. However, if that person becomes isolated
then he will 'exhibit disorders of behaviour, emotion and
thought' (6).

Bureaucratic insensitivity has failed to recognise the existence
of communities as living organisms. The local authorities'
approach to planning has been in the name of progress to destroy
old neighbourhoods in order to eliminate out-of-date buildings;
not recognising that it meant the destruction of true urban
communities. The people who are disrupted are re-settled on
new, sanitised, local authority housing projects in a social and
physical environment which can be strange and foreign. The
problem is that people living in these areas, because of their lack
of money and mobility, are those most in need of informal social
networks with local bases. Both Yancey (7) and Young and
Willmott (8) make the point that there is a class difference in the
need for friends in the same geographic area. Higher classes do not
need a geographically contiguous group of friends because their
informal networks are usually centred on professional and interest
groups which the lower socio-economic classes do not usually
have. The higher classes also have the mobility and inclination to
seek out these other groups which the lower classes often do not.

Many people in urban areas therefore develop a sense of
estrangement from society, and a feeling of powerlessness to
effect social change. It would be wrong to suggest that this sense
results solely from the transplanting of communities. Reasons for
these developments include the evident disorientations of the
Western World in the upheaval of society following World War II.

Zimbardo (9) argues that an individual must see a relationship between his activity and its effects around him. An ability to control one's fate is an essential aspect of behaviour. He warns:

> ... we should not give up our names for more efficient numbers and should resist urban planning which nurtures sterile drab sameness and wipes out neighbourhoods where people are recognised by others and are concerned about the social evaluation of others.

Alienation, hopelessness, violence, aggression and human misery are all related to a physical and/or social environmental condition. These stresses lead to certain types of behavioural abnormalities and disturbances. Some of these abnormalities come to be defined legally as crime and come to the attention of the criminal justice system.

So what can be done to create a sense of social cohesion?

Sociologists' studies have pinpointed a number of factors which help to foster this sense of neighbourhood solidarity. They are:

(a) Physical design of neighbourhoods
(b) Family and community structures
(c) Local relationships
(d) Local values

I believe that the police can assist in creating and/or supporting the above factors by:

(a) Creating communication channels with workers in other statutory agencies and with people living in the community.
(b) Sharing information.
(c) Consulting people before acting.
(d) Encouraging communities to take action for themselves.
(e) Helping to destigmatise areas or communities.

These actions can help to strengthen social cohesion, thereby strengthening informal control systems in several different ways.

They build a variety of relationships ranging from strong and intimate to the multiplex – that is, relationships in which two persons associate in more than one social context. They raise the recognition factor in the neighbourhood. Furthermore, in addition to preventing crime they create aspirations of individual significance, social unity and effective democracy. The following case studies show how they may be given new and appropriate forms of expression.

Case Study 1: Joint Action

A district which gave great concern in Exeter was that of Whipton, on its periphery. In this neighbourhood there are a number of large, modern, local-authority owned housing estates one of which is the Whipton 'Triangle', comprising about 1,600 houses. It is bordered by main roads and railway lines and dominated by Exeter's only block of medium rise flats. In that area there was no neighbourhood association and only two uniformed organisations for youth – Girl Guides and Boys' Brigade – both of which were oversubscribed. Moreover, there was no youth club, though a modern church was fairly well attended, as was a thriving political/social club.

Informal discussions took place between members of the Crime Prevention Support Unit, a county councillor and the Youth and Community Officer. As a result, a joint action group came together representing the church, council, statutory agencies and uniformed organisations. These meetings, taking place over a period of some months, gradually started to turn into a 'talk' shop, with each looking to the other for someone to make a positive move. Such encounters created certain problems for the professionals who took part. One policeman avoided the meetings, finding it difficult to mix with social workers. A social worker found difficulty in discussing community problems with a 'uniformed representative'. There was no doubt that all participants felt that their traditional independence of each other was threatened. All displayed a lack of knowledge of each other's roles. Yet it was agreed that there was an increasing delinquency problem. It was also agreed that the geographical area could be described as a desert in terms of social, cultural and leisure activities; and that a survey should be made of youth and adult needs. This should aim to find out how the youth spent their leisure time and what they wanted in the way of amenities; and also to discover if local adults were aware of local problems. The police surveyed a sample of the adult population, some 118 houses being visited. The Youth and Community Officer surveyed a sample of the youth. Some interesting points emerged.

Adults seemed unaware that there was an increasing trend in delinquency, but they spoke of their feelings of social isolation. They complained about the lack of amenities on or near their estate, being critical of its size and the intention to expand it. Many admitted their inability to cope with their children, being resigned that they would become involved in crime. Some parents saw it as an inevitable problem. Others complained about the remoteness of policemen, social workers and the local authorities. Children spoke of wanting adult involvement in their play and access to recreational facilities. Many of those surveyed only had a social network ranging over three or four streets from their homes. The young people preferred the pub to their parents in their leisure time.

The results of the survey were studied. The vicar was the first to respond by inviting a member of the police unit to speak in his church at a Sunday service about the problems of crime and the need for the community to 'police' itself. Following this service volunteers from the church set up two youth clubs. In addition, with the help of the Youth and Community Officer, a drop-in club was formed for the older youth. A public meeting was called with over 1,000 pamphlets being delivered in a variety of ways. Over 150 people attended the meeting which was held in a local school.

The police talked of the crime trend in the neighbourhood, illustrated by data from our research. The environmental effect on the location of crime was explained by using the local neighbourhood map, so that people could see their crime area. The same technique was used to show their 'juveniles at risk' areas. The city patterns were then revealed, which again emphasised the part which the environment seemed to play in crime. Also shown were the socio-economic indicators and youth outlets in their neighbourhood. The Youth and Community Officer gave a talk on the advantages of recognisable communities working together. He also gave the details of the survey amongst the youth, and explained how he could assist in the formation of a community organisation.

These talks provoked a storm of questions in which no-one escaped criticism. The planners, councillors, police, social workers and even individuals on the estate all came in for some attack. But some people were positive in their response, seeking solutions. A number of people volunteered to help form a community association.

Their names were taken and within a few weeks the second meeting was held with the express purpose of setting up the machinery for the formation of a community association. Under the guidance of the Youth and Community Officer the volunteers carried out a survey to discover the extent of their community as perceived by those living in the area; data was also collated on what activities and organisations already existed in the area and what were needed. Although the original approach was aimed at the local authority housing estate, the local survey showed that the geographical concept of a contiguous community existed across the estate to include the adjoining private housing sector. Eventually, by December 1977, the secretary of the group was able to call his own public meeting for the express purpose of forming a community association. The meeting was well attended and supported by a police representative and the Youth and Community Officer. A talk was given on the purpose of a community association by an organiser of the national federation. The proposal was put to the meeting and adopted, with some eighteen people elected to a number of posts on the committees. The local policeman was elected on the general committee. The committee then began to create initiatives.

One of the first was the community newsletter, circulated around the neighbourhood. It outlined events and activities aimed at specific sectors of the community. For the adults there were the almost obligatory jumble sales and dances plus a community fete, bingo, cheese and wine parties and a 'good-neighbours' scheme. For the young there was a youth club and concert, discos, and summer holday play schemes. Some of the association's activities aimed at counteracting anti-social behaviour by promoting projects such as an anti-litter campaign. They also called a meeting with the specific intention of setting up a youth club run by volunteers to counteract increasing numbers of delinquents. The association raised also over a thousand pounds to purchase 'new ear' equipment for the deaf. These funds came from waste paper collections, the paper being stored in a garage at their local police office. From that time (March 1977) the original few volunteers have gradually built up a community association which is improving life for hundreds of people in the area.

The implementation of pro-active policing meant that volunteers had been able to form a community association with a mandate to improve life in the area. This association was demonstrably growing into a cohesive group. Over the years the Exeter police, like their colleagues in other parts of the country, had become stereotyped in the minds of the public as somewhat traditional in their approach to law and order. The police initiative in Whipton shattered that stereotype.

The Chief Constable was delighted as it confirmed his belief that if given support and responsibility a neighbourhood would want to be involved in countering its own problems of crime and delinquency. In this case he argued it had been achieved because:

1. The police were willing to be flexible and to experiment.
2. The police had identified the problems and were prepared to assist community action.
3. The pro-active measures had brought together a number of statutory agencies – all of whom could, in some way, influence delinquency levels.
4. There had been an analysis of social trends which although 'crude, pragmatic and superficial' nevertheless was sufficiently influential to be catalytic. This analysis had included data from a number of statutory agencies but, most importantly, from the community itself.

Although very pleased with the reaction from the community, the Chief Constable was also aware that this type of activity embarked the police on a course which would involve a considerable philosophical shift from the ideas of policing as traditionally practised. He recognised the difficulties that would be encountered in implementing such a shift. Many entrenched views, both within and outside the police service, had to be influenced and overcome before a movement to communal policing could be effected. The Chief Constable said that these deeply held views were varied and diverse and analysed them thus:

(a) Many policemen regarded the workers in other statutory agencies with considerable scepticism.
(b) There was a natural reluctance or inability in all statutory agencies to recognise or motivate the good in society.
(c) Many workers in other statutory agencies suspected police motives.
(d) Some statutory agency workers saw the 'new' police role encroaching on the territories of other agencies.
(e) Many policemen felt uncomfortable with the image of communal policing because it was not enforcement oriented.

The Chief Constable's analysis was supported in my interviews with other policemen about the Whipton initiative. At a lower level in the police hierarchy was a sergeant who had taken part in the negotiations. He was a member of the Crime Prevention Support Unit. He too, like the Chief Constable, was delighted with the overall reaction from the community and other agencies. He considered that the initial negotiations with the other statutory workers had been protracted due to inexperience, and firmly believed that these could be shortened if the traditional barriers between agencies were lowered. This sergeant was certain that the police had played a crucial role, particularly in the way they had been able to command public support. As he said, 'In the eyes of the public the police have credibility. Whether we deserve this credibility is another argument. We can use our credibility to help other agencies to attain their objectives (such as setting up a community organisation) and a rallying point in the community.'

There were also other components which this CPSU sergeant identified as having assisted in the success. First there was the importance of carrying out a survey which had given the CPSU the community's perspective. He admitted that it changed the police outlook. Secondly, the displayed crime and delinquency data could be easily and widely understood. Thirdly, as the agencies had approached the problem together, action could be co-ordinated across the disciplines. Fourthly, the local politician had decided not to make political capital out of her involvement which might have meant the loss of some volunteers not of her political persuasion. Lastly, the community had been allowed to choose for itself. Although the sergeant was well pleased with the community's response, he witnessed mixed reactions from other policemen who were on the periphery of the initiative.

The varied reactions endorsed the Chief Constable's opinion that many entrenched views would have to be influenced and overcome within the police service before communal policing could be implemented; on the other hand, there were also distinct signs of approbation. In the main, the views about the community project came from three distinct police groups and were biased by their job experiences which influenced their perspectives of the police role. The groups were:

1. Senior police management who were concerned with the implementation of policies and deployment of resources.
2. Policemen who walked neighbourhood beats fulfilling a variety of tasks ranging from pro-active to reactive.
3. Policemen whose main task was to drive police cars (panda, incident and traffic vehicles) thereby fulfilling the essential fire-brigade tasks of policing.

One senior police officer reacted to the project by expressing reservations about crime data being released to the public and suggested it was a possible breach of the Official Secrets Act. His concern was echoed by other senior officers in the division, who thought that the police did not have the resources, particularly manpower, to be able to initiate other community-based projects as in Whipton. Another senior officer argued that it was an abdication of the traditional law enforcement role in favour of one based on humane policies which would, in time, lead to a weakening of police authority in the neighbourhood. One superintendent expressed a minority point of view in saying that 'law keeping is a community task. The police are the professionals and must take a lead in the community by encouraging a collective conscience to fight delinquency. This can only be achieved if we are part of the community.'

It was amongst the constables who walked the beat and rode in cars that views were found which were diametrically opposed.

The constable who worked on foot in this part of Whipton initially viewed the work of the CPSU with trepidation, for the following reasons:

1. A fear that he would lose stature in the eyes of the community if he was seen participating in a 'soft' police project.
2. A fear that his police training and experience had not equipped him to develop or support community action.
3. That there was little or no encouragement from his own supervisory officers to attend the inter-agency preliminary meetings, partly because the police were clearly represented by the CPSU.
4. That he found it difficult to understand how an inter-agency team could work together because of the cynical attitudes of professionals from different disciplines towards each other.
5. That the CPSU had insisted that a questionnaire should be administered in the community to discover what the people thought about his policing and other local matters.
6. That the people in the neighbourhood would reject the idea, and that the effort would therefore be wasted.

To his delight he found that his required active participation in the growth and development of the community association ensured that these fears quickly disappeared. First, the constable became convinced that his stature in the community had been enhanced because he was seen in both a pro-active and reactive role. His ability to play both roles had resulted in his social network of formal and informal contacts being considerably enlarged, thus making his job easier. To his surprise he had found that his previous police experience helped him in his pro-active role. This experience stemmed from his ability to relate to people and the lessons learnt from the everyday occurrences he had dealt with in his career; being accepted as an 'official' adjudicator in domestic problems; his intimate knowledge of community life and his willingness to exercise discretionary powers. On the other hand he emphasised that with some training in public speaking and committee work and with greater knowledge of the criteria for community involvement, he could have made a greater contribution.

Police management was also now more positive in encouraging

him to participate in the association's affairs and other local events. This came about because, after the association's formation, the CPSU withdrew, leaving him 'holding the baby'. Now if problems arose or he needed help then he telephoned the CPSU who invariably gave suitable assistance. This ranged from printing posters to arranging displays at a fete. The example set by the original inter-agency team ensured that a close relationship developed between the different grass-root workers in the area, and this led to closer formal and informal consultation. His worries about the questionnaire had subsided because its findings had resulted in the statutory agencies, particularly the police, trying to improve the quality of service that they gave to the neighbour-hood. Lastly, he admitted amazement at the way the association had developed from the efforts of the original few volunteers. Its range of activities covered a wide spectrum of human interests with one common thread, that all led to improvement in the community's quality of life. He sensed a different mood in the neighbourhood. Because of his personal involvement in the project and the benefits that were accruing, not only to himself but also to the people, the constable was now committed to pro-active policing. The experience had changed his attitude.

A different version was given by policemen driving panda cars. After witnessing the implementation of the scheme, one young panda car driver said that it filled him with dismay and concern as it was obvious that the police were acting outside their traditional role. He thought that pro-active work was the province of the social worker, youth leader and other statutory agencies. It was these agencies which should have been developing the pro-active concept, since a main causal factor in the alarming increase in crime in recent years was their growing ineffectiveness. He was quite emphatic that the police service could not afford to have a policeman attending community meetings, let alone encouraging the public to set up a community organisation, because the present level of police manpower was quite insufficient to deal with their present reactive tasks. The only solution to neighbourhoods like Whipton was to raise the level of uniform patrols both on foot and by car, coupled with the strict interpretation and enforcement of the law. Furthermore it was morally wrong of the Chief

Constable and the CPSU to go around claiming that the Whipton project was a success without being able to produce figures showing a substantial decrease in the recorded levels of criminality. He claimed that there had been no change in the area as a result of the community association's activities – if anything he had more work than before.

The sentiments expressed by the Exeter policemen about the project were mixed on the merits of pro-active policing. In contrast, there was unanimous agreement amongst the statutory agency workers at all levels. They wholeheartedly supported the overall concept and considered the Whipton project to be a resounding success. A representative social worker remarked on the improved levels of communication which had been achieved with the policeman who covered the area. This had led to a far better exchange of information, and a bond of trust was developing. He recalled that during the inter-agency meetings he thought the CPSU policemen were being rather 'pushy' and in a hurry to accomplish the project without having much idea about the objectives. He recalled that they had been obsessed with calling a public meeting and that they had made a vague threat to go it alone if the rest of the group did not agree. On several occasions during these preliminary meetings he had been worried by policemen's apparent lack of sensitivity about community feelings. For instance, they had insisted right from the start that it was their intention to reveal the neighbourhood delinquency spot map. Paradoxically, at the public meetings the police spokesman had presented the data very sensitively, explaining that much delinquency was the product of urban environment; of lack of leisure facilities; of lack of community activity; of lack of parental control; of the opportunities for crime and the high numbers of children in certain neighbourhoods. Even so, the social worker still had some reservations about releasing such data because he feared it could be wrongly interpreted, thus causing even greater stigmatisation.

The social worker also thought that the policemen and youth and community officer had conducted the public meeting with imagination and firmness in handling the audience's questions. The 'bring back capital punishment' and 'bring back the birch' supporters were given little scope and the people were turned away from these unobtainable solutions to more constructive ones which they could achieve. Taking all things into consideration, the social worker thought the project a success because the inter-agency team had agreed on a catalytic role which had led the community to accept increased responsibility.

The Exeter Youth and Community Officer approved the project and saw five important stages in its construction.

1. Statutory agencies had met and exchanged relevant statistical information.
2. The inter-agency team had co-ordinated action.
3. Surveys had been carried out by the police and his own department to obtain the community's perspectives.
4. The public meeting had given the community its chance to choose its own course of action.
5. The first few volunteers with the help of his department had developed a thriving community association which was working amongst the neighbourhood's youth, old people, the disabled and disadvantaged.

The Youth Officer recognised that the police action in releasing the spot-map data to the statutory agencies and other community representatives (local politicians and churchmen), had prompted the inter-agency meeting which led to the formation of the team. However, whilst he thought police involvement to be crucial, he thought their role should be limited. It was crucial because the way the police had used data lent an air of urgency to the problem; and because his experience in Exeter showed that the police had the ability to command public attention.

He supported this statement by comparing the number of people who had turned out to police/public meetings as compared to his own. Hundreds had attended the police meetings while, on some occasions, his own agency only attracted single numbers.

The police role should nevertheless be limited because: some people would see police involvement as 'smacking of the heavy hand of the authority'; some policemen tended to ignore local government bureaucracy, thereby causing offence and hostility; some policemen were insensitive to the views held by other statutory workers who were more professional and experienced in community work; and some police statements and actions had shown a limited knowledge of theory behind community work.

Local politicians who had taken an interest in the project right from the start admitted that it was the police action in releasing the crime data that had prompted them to action. They considered that the inter-agency meetings had dragged on but put this down to the inexperience of the various disciplines in working together. They had been astounded at the number of people who had turned up at the public meeting. They had at first thought it unfortunate that one of them had not been allowed to chair the meeting because the police Superintendent had said it might mean the loss of some volunteers who would not come forward because of their political views; and that as the police had been instrumental in calling the meeting (using police posters in schools, churches and local shops), under no circumstances would he allow it to be chaired by a politician.

They thought the Superintendent was too rigid, but in view of his attitude they had reluctantly stepped down. During the public meeting, however, and much to their surprise, the Superintendent had publicly complimented them on the positive contribution they had made in working with the inter-agency team. The whole experience, and the subsequent growth of the community association with police involvement and support, finally caused them to endorse fully the concept of pro-active policing.

This endorsement was wholly supported by one of the original volunteers who helped form the community association. Prior to attending the public meeting this young woman had never had any contact with the police until a pamphlet was delivered by the local newsboy. In this CPSU pamphlet she read that the police were calling a public meeting to reveal facts on crime and delinquency. The proposed meeting became a talking point amongst her neighbours and several agreed to go to the local school because 'we were intrigued to know more about our neighbourhood'. She was amazed that over 200 other people attended, not only from the council estate but also from the surrounding private housing sector. The police Superintendent encouraged the people to air their grievances about the service given by police, and showed maps using an overhead projector. This lady found the spot-maps difficult to understand because of a small screen and the size of the audience. It was not until later in a much smaller group that she was able to study the statistical points presented. Three main points emerged about the police. The first was that only a few people knew or saw the local policeman, even though he was supposed to be a local beat officer. Secondly, people felt they were not getting a good service from the police. Their main complaint was that minor public disorders (i.e. domestic disputes and rowdy youngsters) were not adequately dealt with and this left them feeling insecure and isolated. The third and probably the most important point was that the police were not aware of a lot of petty crime, vandalism and delinquency that took place, and even if the police did take action no-one ever knew the outcome.

There was a general call for more policemen in the area, though it was obvious from the questions and answers that people were hesitant about the role they wanted the police to play. The police Superintendent made it clear that more policemen could not cure the community's rising delinquency level; and the lady began to realise that the community could deal with some of its own problems in ways such as schemes to divert youngsters from petty crime. On the other hand there was a need for the community to support the police so they could detect the more serious crime. It was this argument that 'won' her over to volunteering to help form the community association.

The original few volunteers suffered from a lack of administrative experience. Although they came from varying socio-economic backgrounds no-one really understood how committees worked, or the need for agendas, minutes and financial records. She thought the professional agencies could have helped more and simplified some of the procedures. For instance, the rules setting up the association were far too complex for most of them to understand. The local policeman was delegated to help the group. Although willing, with a very pleasant personality, they found him to be nervous and, like themselves, lacking in organisational expertise. As the meetings went by he gained confidence, becoming a great help by offering sound advice and support. Because of his relationship with the community association a positive bond was formed between him and the local people. This meant more work for him. As a volunteer said, 'when the local drunk tried to ride his motor cycle up the flat staircase we were quick to ring for the police. We would never have done that before. We feel we can now. They dealt with it easily and it quietened the drunk down for a little while.' She was certain that the community association would not have got off the ground had it not been for the police calling the meeting. She thought the police image charismatic, and it was this that had attracted the large audience. The roles of the other social agencies such as social services and youth workers were little known to the general public.

The volunteer was positive that the community had, by forming the association, helped to prevent crime. Her reasons were:

1. The association's activities had resulted in a number of outlets being formed for youth such as discos, youth clubs, and a youth concert. These events had attracted a lot of support and at least whilst they were going on some youngsters would have been diverted from crime.
2. The youth activities were run by a cross-section of well meaning local people and it was hoped that some young people who had problems or came from problem families would be able to talk about them with the local helpers in a more meaningful way than with a paid local government worker.
3. The various activities had brought together people from all walks of life; many were strangers to each other and new relationships were formed. Raising the level of recognition amongst people ensured a release in the tensions which so often caused family violence, particularly amongst the young married women who were isolated on the estate, tied down by poverty or their family commitments.

She thought the fundamental objective of the association was to be a voice of the people of Whipton to air their views and opinions and to serve community needs by providing activities. The prevention of crime was a 'spin-off' from their activities. The volunteer suggested that its formation had brought together people from all walks of life and that the association was made up of a good mix of people from both council and private housing. This, in her mind, made the project a successful co-operative venture, fusing police and community together in a bond which was leading to feelings of security, stability and the ability to communicate.

An examination of the views expressed by the witnesses revealed areas of agreement and disagreement. First was the importance of the role that crime data can play. The agency representatives saw it performing a catalytic function 'jerking them out of their complacency'; equally it served as a bridge between the agencies, bonding them together with a common interest. Second was the general agreement on the importance of inter-agency co-operation as crime could be prevented by harmonising the work of statutory agencies. Third was the accep- tance that the community itself must tackle the problem of preventing minor crime and delinquency. There was some dis- agreement as to whether the police should involve themselves positively in a non-conflict social role. On the one hand there were the arguments against: that policemen lacked sensitivity in community affairs; and that the police service lacked sufficient resources to 'indulge' in social crime prevention.

The policemen who took part in the project and the local volunteer thought otherwise; they saw the police involvement as an essential contribution, though it would have been improved if those involved had greater knowledge of committee organisation.

Case Study 2: Unilateral Action

The following projects also show how the police can help to reinforce social control. Unlike the previously described Whipton project in which the police worked with other agencies, here the police decided to go it alone by starting a recreational scheme for young people. This direct action created suspicion amongst other agency workers and the public because there was a failure to consult or inform. In some ways it lent support to the critics who accused the police of possessing little or no experience in community work practices. On the other hand it could be argued that imaginative action is catalytic, firing others to action.

An idea by the then Deputy Chief Constable, John Woodcock (now Chief Constable of South Wales) was put to the Crime Prevention Support Unit, that we should consider new initiatives for young people. As he said, analysis had pointed to a need to activate the community or the agencies into creating leisure opportunities for the young in these neighbourhoods. A survey was made of the city to find out where young people played or congregated. It showed that although Exeter had plenty of green open spaces which were especially near or adjoining most of the 'juveniles at risk' areas, little activity took place on or in them. It was found that the green spaces were used more frequently by middle-aged people exercising their dogs than children exercising their bodies. With some trepidation the members of the Unit decided to set up recreational activities in two different parts of the city. Permission was granted by the Exeter City Council for the Unit to organise games and activities in their parks and playing fields.

The first area chosen was Barton Fields, Exeter, which is a large playing field surrounded by a variety of housing environments, ranging from low-profile local authority owned flats to terrace-type houses of early twentieth-century construction with very small gardens or yards. After going through the traumatic experience of exchanging their uniforms for tracksuits, members of the Crime Prevention Support Unit visited these playing fields over a period of thirteen weeks. A number of activities were offered, such as soccer, rugby and a variety of other games. Specific nights were police-oriented, with visits by the police handler and his dog, police motor cyclists, police cars, and even the Police Band. The numbers of young people attending rose from ten to 300 a night with ages ranging from three to eighteen years. This was accomplished by word of mouth advertising to avoid being swamped by a deluge of caring parents from the other parts of the city seeking to involve their 'nice' children in what was after all an attractive recreational scheme.

It was found that different age groups could play in competition without resorting to violence. Their respect for each other was demonstrated by the fact that one of the most popular young people was a disabled boy who was confined to a wheelchair. They continually insisted that he must and did participate in their game.

The intention was to keep things going in the area by getting the parents involved. To achieve this, notes were sent home by the children inviting them to come along to meet the policemen. At first a few parents attended, standing in isolated groups, but were brought together and told in an informal way the purpose of the police scheme. Later at a meeting they were shown the empirical data. The parents responded and gradually took over the scheme, running it themselves with the help of their resident policeman.

This policeman had initially shown reluctance to become involved with the track-suited policemen from Headquarters, but within weeks he became very committed to the scheme. He requested and got his own track-suit. This came about because of the informal pressure from local people and children. Since that summer he has extended the scheme to every school holiday excluding half-terms. Up to 120 young people are catered for during morning sessions which are held on local authority property. An open invitation had also been circulated to all policemen in the city, but it was only the resident constables who came forward to make any contribution. The comments of other policemen ranged from abuse to cynical amusement.

A second scheme took place at Bettysmead playing fields which is surrounded by pre-war housing. Most of the housing belongs to the local authority or a housing association. It is a 'juveniles at risk' area. Again the same activities were offered to the young people over a period of thirteen weeks. The ages of those who attended were about the same as in the other scheme, with a regular attendance of about 100. Many lessons were learnt from it. It was found that children had difficulty in playing together without resorting to arguments, cursing, swearing and fighting. The factions from the different types of housing would instantly divide for any team game, which helped to fuel the tension. Experience taught us that they had to be mixed. But, by the end of the summer, we were noticing a change for the better in the young people's attitudes towards each other and also towards the police. The older ones were beginning to take over the refereeing of some of the games; though on more than one occasion, small groups would be seen leaving the playing fields to settle their differences in the usual physical fashion away from our scrutiny.

Efforts to activate adults in the area brought little or no response. The few who came forward took one look at what we were trying to do, and left. By the end of the summer the Bettysmead activity scheme had no adults to support it.

The Youth and Community Service had taken an early interest in our two activity schemes and offered (which was gladly accepted) to take over the Bettysmead scheme, using locally unemployed people. Since then they have extended the scheme into other 'juveniles at risk' areas in the city. They now believe that they have a responsibility to take their resources into the estates.

Last summer (1980) the number of holiday play schemes in Exeter produced over 5,000 places for young people. They covered a wide range of activity ranging from handicraft to canoeing. The total project is co-ordinated by the Youth and Community Officer and organised and run by a mixture of agency workers and volunteers.

The schemes have also been copied by parents on two other large local authority housing estates in Exeter. Both these estates have a regular pattern of reported petty crime and juvenile delinquency, especially during their summer school holidays. Parents in these two neighbourhoods expressed concern when they saw the empirical evidence. They were offered the support of a local policeman who, with the assistance of the Youth and Community Service, obtained such facilities as a hall or play area, sports equipment and painting material for them to run their own recreational schemes. This they did on several days of each week for the duration of the summer holidays. During these holidays no crimes were reported to the police as being committed in these communities. Comparisons with the same periods in previous years showed regular reports of crime in the past in those neighbourhoods. But it should be made clear that the Crime Prevention Support Unit have never claimed that these recreational schemes in themselves prevented crime; this phenomenon is open to all kinds of interpretation. Some academics have suggested that delinquency is a form of play; and perhaps the play schemes are simply substitutes.

It is difficult to say who learnt most from these non-conflict contacts between young people and policemen. The experiences made us all reflect. Young people cheering policemen getting out of a white Land Rover; a young boy pouring out his troubles about being with policemen when his two brothers were in prison; a young boy who could only express his thoughts about policemen as 'Bloody fuzz, because that's what my dad calls you'; and the immortal saying from a twelve year old: 'Mister, until you came here with that bloody whistle, it was chaos'.

A local resident constable summed up the benefits of such schemes (10):

There are undoubtedly many spin-offs to my advantage as resident Police Constable. For example I have now developed an extremely good liaison with the Headmistress, staff and pupils at Union Street School. Also I have obviously developed a very close relationship with the members of the activity scheme who all live in my area . . . It is with these children that I think the earliest measures of improved relationships are noted. Young children attending Union Street School today will, in 7 or 8 years, be the senior pupils in St Thomas High School, the most difficult of all age groups – could it be that these friendly talks and encounters with their local policeman will bear fruit in years to come when the school leavers are making their presence felt in society? I think it is necessary for all policemen in my position to have the hope that by gaining the confidence of the young children and breaking down this barrier of conflict, which undoubtedly exists in the older ones, then perhaps in some small way we are making Exeter a better place to live in in the future. If the conventional methods of policing do not appear to have worked perhaps it is right that we give this new policy an opportunity to prove itself. It is not always easy for a policeman with several years service to change his role overnight to encompass the work of community workers. Most policemen, trained and encouraged into a more positive attitude towards crime and anti-social behaviour, find preventive policing alien to their natural inclination. I think I am fortunate in this respect in that I have not found this transition too difficult. Possibly having two children at the local school has had a moderating influence in my attitude towards the younger generation.

His remarks are, in some measure, supported by a young policeman who drove a panda car in the same area. Initially he had been alarmed at the scheme, maintaining that it was not the role of the police to be running recreational schemes for young people. It was an infringement of other people's roles. Then an experience caused him reluctantly to change his mind. What convinced him was listening to his resident constable colleague speak about the scheme's advantages, and being in his presence whilst on duty at a local football match where a gang of football supporters cheered his colleague by name. It appeared that these supporters regularly attended the officer's recreational scheme. As a result, he too started to help out and by direct experience of the scheme finally became convinced of its usefulness.

However, many other policemen in Exeter were unconvinced. A senior officer approaching the end of his service queried what the public reaction would be if they knew that policemen were engaged on such duties instead of investigating crime. He saw the whole exercise as a publicity gimmick. His remarks were echoed by a local policeman who walked the beat. This very experienced constable, who is highly respected by his own community with whom he has worked for eight years, was convinced that if he participated in games with the young people on his estate, it would lead to him losing authority and the youth would increasingly take advantage of him. He fully supported the need for such activities to counteract delinquency but said that it must be initiated by the people in the community or by other local authority workers.

A youth leader also thought the police recreational projects of limited value. He complained that the police had failed to tap his expertise, and that he had only heard of the projects through the media. Because he had not been invited he had not bothered to visit them. He also had doubts about some policemen's ability to relate to young people. He recalled that he had once had the help of eight police volunteers, and had found that four had great difficulty in talking to young people. This caused him to question the usefulness of such projects as the policemen could end up doing more harm than good. As he remarked: 'If they can't talk to kids while they are playing with them what chance have they of talking to those wandering the streets or messing about at football matches?'

His third criticism was that even the policemen whom he had trained in youth work occasionally resorted to authoritarian methods to accomplish their pro-active task. He quoted an example of a policeman who was a trained youth leader taking over a youth club with a reputation for noisy behaviour. Within a few weeks the 'rowdies' had left because they would not accept the policeman's discipline. His fourth and final criticism was that as the policemen had been unable to attract parental support, his department had needed to take it on, using unemployed people. He thought that by building up expectations they were unable to satisfy, the police had done their image more harm than good.

A social worker in her early twenties also spoke of her initial reservations about the project, believing it to be just another 'Alderson publicity gimmick'. As far as she was concerned, the police lacked the necessary skills to be able to influence behavioural patterns in a positive way. Although the social workers had been invited, she refused to visit the playing fields project because she did not want to be seen giving support to 'cosmetic surgery'. Later she regretted this refusal because a number of young people, particularly one of her own clients, gave unsolicited support for the scheme. These young people said that the experience was fun and kept them out of trouble. It was the police involvement that had given the project an air of excitement. They had visits by policemen in traffic cars, panda cars, dog vans, and even the band. The discipline had been fairly strict and on more than one occasion when things had got out of hand, the policemen had just packed up and left, though they always turned up the following week.

The social worker said that these experiences had amused her but also caused her to reflect on her own attitudes, and to drop any reservations about the scheme except that the policemen should be careful not to impose their own middle-class standards on these 'deprived children'.

A volunteer in her early thirties who had participated in the Barton Field scheme was fulsome in her praise. Her only criticism was that the people in the neighbourhood should have been pre-warned about the project as on the night it started she rang the police station to report 'some men are enticing children into the playing field by posing as policemen'! The scheme caused considerable comment throughout the neighbourhood; people were at first puzzled and suspicious about the motive behind it. Her own involvement started when her children brought home a note from the policemen inviting parents to visit the scheme and to talk with them. She visited the playing fields and met the policemen who gave a variety of reasons for carrying out the project:

1. To combat rising delinquency in new ways.
2. To show that recreational activities can bring local people together in useful ways.
3. To emphasise the responsibilities of parents.
4. To improve relationships between police and local people.

Even on her first visit the policemen got her involved in games. As far as she was concerned the project achieved its objectives, but there were also other benefits which she had witnessed. People in the same street who had been strangers to each other were now talking and relating. The police had built on this new relationship by bringing the people together to meet their local policemen and discuss local problems. These meetings culminated each year in a visit to the licensed police club which was seen as *the* event. Another benefit was that sporting clubs such as the local rugby club visited the project and creamed off likely candidates for their own sport. In addition, her own children enjoyed the project so much that she was able to use it as a reward/punishment. The project became a common focal point where people of all ages came to be entertained or to participate; and local children now used the playing fields far more than they had done in the past.

She went on to explain that now she, with other volunteers, ran similar schemes each school holiday with the support of the local policeman. Her one criticism was that they were not always supported by local parents – they often opted out and the number of volunteers tended to fluctuate alarmingly. She thought the policeman ought to spend more time pressurising local people instead of doing everything himself. As a result of her involvement, she and other volunteers now knew hundreds of youngsters in the area. All in all, she considered the project had improved the quality of life in the neighbourhood.

The following year a similar project run by a local youth leader on the other side of the playing field had little effect, because many of the children were unaware of its existence. Those who attended found that it lacked excitement with no end product. But the police project had resulted in many more people knowing each other. More importantly, they all knew their policemen. In consequence, the volunteer had developed a great sense of respect for the police which she admitted was non-existent before the scheme started. She was certain that in the long term delinquent behaviour in the neighbourhood would decrease because of the new relationship.

In sum, reactions to the police initiatives varied, with greater approval coming from those who participated most fully. Within the CPSU there was general pleasure at the success of the initiatives, but even here, divisions of opinion as to future policy. On the one hand there was the argument that the problems of trying to work closely with other statutory agencies were insurmountable. These agencies often seemed to lack initiative and enthusiasm, and showed a marked reluctance to do anything unless extra funds were forthcoming. More importantly, their continual suspicion and questioning of police motives caused feelings of hostility. As a result, there was a demand to pursue 'police only' initiatives. The recreational scheme was quoted to support this argument. The counter argument was that pro-active policing could only be truly effective if it developed agency co-operation and co-ordination. The Whipton project was quoted to support this argument. The next chapter describes how the CPSU resolved this dilemma.

4. The Formation of the Exeter Policing Consultative Group

The relative success of both the unilateral and joint projects described in the last chapter posed a central question for the CPSU. Should it concentrate its efforts on going it alone or on collaborating with other agencies? In reflecting on this dilemma one point finally helped swing it in favour of the latter, namely the results of the patterns of crime and delinquency. It was apparent that no one statutory agency held the answer to crime, though each was capable of making some contribution. Thus, the CPSU concluded that if agencies co-ordinated their actions, far more crime would be prevented than if the police acted alone.

The evidence of the Exeter crime and juvenile delinquency patterns clearly showed that other agencies' policies influenced levels of criminality. Agencies such as housing, planning, education and others all had their effects but were they aware of the fact? At that time in 1976 and 1977 liaison between police divisions and the agencies at both county and district level was negligible, and only took place where statute demanded it or at time of crisis. Moreover, the CPSU experiences showed the difficulties that they would encounter in setting up co-ordinating machinery. Recurring problems of confidentiality, suspicion, jealousy and 'what's in it for me?' attitudes existing between agencies would have to be overcome; and if not overcome, at least prevented from becoming insurmountable barriers to co-operation.

It was decided to tackle these problems in a variety of ways:

1. The CPSU approached the Social and Probation Services and arranged for policemen to be attached to them for one week. So successful were these attachments that the other services requested reciprocal arrangements with the police.
2. The CPSU arranged and encouraged formal and informal contacts with other agencies with particular emphasis on the latter.
3. The CPSU offered their resources (manpower and/or equipment) to help other agencies.

4. The CPSU offered the results of their analysis to other agencies.

In brief, what emerged was a growing pattern of collaboration. Therefore, the next main issue was whether or not to make this a formal structure.

As a result the idea of forming a structure was generally aired. It was suggested that a neighbourhood be selected and steps taken to improve its quality of life, in particular to reduce its crime.

The representatives gave support to the idea and seemed generally sympathetic, although no one seemed willing to give a lead. The CPSU therefore decided to call together representatives of eighteen different agencies to form a consultative group, preceding this with a series of meetings of key agencies: Social Services, Education, Youth and Community, and Probation. In the course of these preliminary discussions the following objectives were suggested which were later adopted by the main consultative group.

1. To provide a forum for sharing respective problems and initiatives.
2. To identify community needs and to formulate possible action through a multi-discipline approach and to report where necessary to appropriate bodies.
3. To maximise the use of available resources.
4. To review, support and monitor local community initiatives.
5. To determine and promote a training programme for a multi-discipline approach.

Later the first objective was changed as follows: 'To provide a community forum for considering ways in which to reduce crime by social as well as police action and for sharing our respective problems and initiatives.'

A letter signed by the Chief Constable was then sent to representatives of the following agencies inviting them to attend a meeting at police Headquarters:

Probation	District Health Authority
Employment	Social Services
Youth and Community	Magistrates
County Council	Press

City Leisure Committee
Department of Health and Social
   Security
Education
Planning
Community Service Volunteers

Engineers
Transport
Housing
Council of Churches
City Council

The CPSU also decided to invite a representative from the National Association for the Care and Resettlement of Offenders (NACRO) to observe the proceedings. It was felt that an observer from outside the area would be able to give an unbiased account of the proceedings without fear of offending anyone. NACRO seemed to fulfil these requirements, being involved itself in research into different aspects of crime prevention. A detailed NACRO report was published on the first twelve months' workings of the group in 1979 (1).

The letter explained that the aim of the meeting was to consider establishing an advisory panel to promote social crime prevention at grass-roots level in defined areas of Exeter. Everyone accepted the invitation and the meeting lasted a day. It was split into two parts. The morning was given to five speakers who were (a) the Chief Constable (b) a Chief Superintendent (c) a University Lecturer (d) the City Planning Officer and (e) the Superintendent of the Crime Prevention Support Unit. The afternoon session took the form of discussions in small groups inviting suggestions on how the group could help remedy the problems of a selected city neighbourhood. Then followed a plenary session on the advantages that could accrue from co-ordination of resources.

The meeting was opened by the Chief Constable who outlined his policing philosophy and suggested ways in which the task of combating crime and delinquency could act as a focus for inter-agency co-operation to improve the quality of life in local communities. 'Was there not a need for some form of advisory group which would lead to the sharing of ideas, resources and initiatives?' he asked.

After other speakers had given their views on local problems and on the influence of social and environmental factors on crime, the CPSU Superintendent presented his Unit's analysis of local crime and offender areas. Commerce, transport, leisure facilities, allocation of houses and planning were identified as factors influencing crime and offender levels. Examples quoted included the ways in which commercial incentives to promote impulse buying had also led to impulse stealing; and the effects of stopping buses at 10.45 p.m. whilst the pubs stayed open until 11.15 p.m. at weekends, which had led to crime patterns between the city centre and housing estates.

The CPSU Superintendent went on to show that each month 75% of crime fell within the same priority areas. It was this predictability that demonstrated how little influence police alone had on overall crime, and the importance of other factors outside police control.

Other examples were given concerning streets which the CPSU had designated as 'juveniles at risk' areas. Some 60% of young people coming to the notice of the police were from these designated areas, which were mostly council estates. The Superintendent suggested that here were the most appropriate areas for agencies to work together, sharing data and responding to the communities' views before implementing new services.

At the end of the plenary session the Youth and Community Officer proposed the formation of a consultative group called the Exeter Policing Consultative Group. This was approved and a steering committee was nominated with the following representatives:

Youth and Community Officer
Senior Probation Officer
Divisional Director of Social Services
Vice-Chairman of City Leisure Committee
Area Education Officer
Administrator of the Exeter Health District
Secretary of the Exeter City CSV
Police Superintendent (CPSU)

The development of the consultative group was slow and at times hesitant, not unexpected in view of its lack of experience in co-operative matters and the lack of a similar model elsewhere.

The first crisis developed slowly over a series of meetings and erupted when the City Housing Officer and the Planning

Research Officer wrote to the Steering Committee accusing it of shortcomings:

1. Its lack of firm decision making.
2. Its failure to formulate policies for a joint approach.
3. The lack of consultation with the public.
4. The lack of consultation with grass-root workers.
5. Its failure to co-ordinate research.

They proposed:

(a) A series of meetings throughout Exeter to discover needs, at which the police should adopt a low profile.
(b) The need to drop the word 'Policing' from the group's title.
(c) The need to brief all grass-root workers in Exeter to strengthen liaison.

The tone of this letter jolted the CPSU into action and a sergeant was deputed to liaise with all members of the committee. An examination of the committee's structure also revealed that the police had been trying to do too much and that the time had come for work to be shared around. As a result, the following structure was agreed upon.

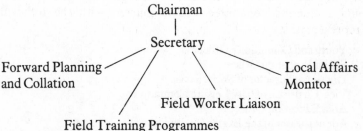

Chairman

Secretary

Forward Planning and Collation

Local Affairs Monitor

Field Worker Liaison

Field Training Programmes

The Planning Research Officer took on the task of Forward Planning and Collation of data. His functions are described later in this chapter.

The task of co-ordinating a training programme was taken on by the Youth and Community Officer. Lack of knowledge as to what joint action teams needed in the way of training meant that expertise could only be acquired slowly by experimenting and evaluating the results.

The third task, that of Field Worker Liaison, was taken on by the City Housing Officer who was to ensure that local field worker groups met their objectives.

The fourth task devised was that of Local Affairs Monitor. Again, the committee agreed that it wanted to be kept informed of the local authority's plans and policies so that they would be able to give suitable advice. This role was taken on by the councillor who was admirably suited by virtue of his position and commitment to the concept.

The secretary's job went to the police sergeant who had spent so much time getting the committee back on course; the chairmanship stayed with the Police Chief Superintendent. To demonstrate their good intentions the police suggested that the chairmanship should be shared around. Most of the other representatives were uncertain about this suggestion but local politicians were adamant that the police should retain the chair. They made two points. First, that they would not sit on a steering committee if the chairman was one of their local authority officers who normally worked under their direction. Secondly, that police political neutrality was above suspicion, whereas they had doubts about some local authority workers.

These modifications were accepted and overcame the criticisms expressed by the City Housing Officer and the Planning Research Officer. Although there had been fears of the police dominating the proceedings, now that everyone was participating in some way or other the fears seemed to be allayed.

The second crisis was not of such intensity. It arose out of each agency's reluctance to share data. There were also administrative difficulties because there were no common boundaries. A research officer in the Planning Department explored various possibilities and eventually decided on sub-dividing the city into areas of similar overall character. The 1971 census had revealed that household type correlated well to overall house type. The city was therefore zoned by defining physically separate areas of different housing, i.e. local authority, large detached, Victorian terraced and so on. The final number of zones from 1,200 streets was fifty-eight. The research officer also ensured that the zones could be amalgamated into ward totals.

The next problem that he faced was in ascertaining what items of information the agencies would contribute. Each agency produced different requirements and had a different potential for supplying information. Some had research sections which were used to supplying data while others did not keep any statistics. The research officer's work on zoning meant that each agency now possessed a common basis. Agreement was reached that a number of agencies would endeavour to produce their own information for 1978. After collection of this information it would then be possible to display it visually to determine the spatial distribution of the various items. This comparative analysis meant that the consultative group would be able to decide on the neighbourhoods that needed its attention.

Information was gathered from:

Police – who provided records of reported crimes by location, of offence and the type of crime – the location of juvenile offenders by age, sex and crime for which reported – the relationship between crime committed and the location of offenders.

Probation – age, sex and category of offence or problem.

Social services – referrals – service requested – case loads – client age and household.

Housing – transfer requests – incidents of rent paid by DHSS.

Consultations were still being carried out with other agencies such as the Department of Health, the Social Services and Education. Many of these agencies were extremely anxious as to whether such information should be shared or revealed. However, confidentiality was protected as all data was based on the fifty-eight zones and therefore no individual householder could be identified. Furthermore, the local Planning Officer had responsibility for co-ordinating all the data, thus obviating the suspicion that the police were responsible. Even this protection did not stop well meaning but misinformed people ringing national newspapers such as *The Guardian* and also the local newspaper, complaining that the Exeter Police were building up data banks on every person living within the city.

The peak achievements were (i) the creation of a joint training programme; and (ii) the development of a general advisory role.

The *first* derived from the consultative group's pilot scheme on ways to improve life in St Thomas, Exeter. St Thomas has a number of different housing areas but two were causing concern. The first was a new 'first time' private owner housing estate called Exwick, built up by a number of developers over a period of a few years. There were few facilities such as public transport, meeting places or play areas. The Social Services admitted that they were already visiting a larger than average number of families in the area. This large sprawling housing estate also had a high proportion of young children who might be at risk within two or three years. The committee agreed that these factors singled it out as an ideal area in which to start preventive initiatives.

The other area of concern in St Thomas was a small pre-war local authority housing estate called Buddle Lane. Analysis showed that this small area had had, over the past three years, a sharp increase in the number of young people coming to the notice of the police for assault, burglary, theft and damage. The numbers were: 1974 – 15; 1975 – 22; 1976 – 34; 1977 – 48 +.

The two neighbourhoods were different in many ways:

Exwick
Private ownership
Well kept houses and gardens
Garage parking

Buddle Lane
Rented local authority accommodation
Drab houses with occasional unkept gardens
On the road parking

The steering committee decided that the first task other than collating data was to bring together the field workers. Not wanting these workers to go through a long drawn-out process of getting to know each other, the police proposed a one-day joint training programme for them. The proposal was accepted and with some guidance from the other representatives the police set up a pilot project at Police Headquarters. The objectives were:

1. To get the different agency workers to meet.
2. To learn about each other's roles.
3. To appreciate difference of role.
4. To discuss mutual problems.
5. To develop mutual respect.
6. To plan future strategies.

The following representatives attended:

Police constables – 2; Police sergeant – 1; Social workers – 2; Youth and Community workers – 4; Teachers – 4; Councillor – 1; Housing Officer – 1; Planners – 2; Voluntary associate (Probation Service) – 1.

Specific members of the steering group (Police, Health, Housing, Social Services and Youth and Community) gave talks on the objectives and tasks of their own particular agency. The workers were then split into two groups depending on the area in which they worked, and given an exercise in which they had to propose improvements to the overall quality of life in their respective areas by maximising existing resources and avoiding duplication of effort.

The whole exercise became somewhat confused because the organiser (a CPSU officer) made too many and too ill-defined demands on the group. The group failed to meet those demands, but thought they had gained a great deal in creating new relationships. Thus though the CPSU were disappointed, the exercise resulted in groups of field workers starting to meet regularly in their own neighbourhoods.

After this the task of training was taken over by the Youth and Community Officer who has since organised two joint agency exercises which have brought neighbourhood field workers together. The exercises took place well outside Exeter in a Dartmoor hostel where the workers participated in a programme about family, community and aspects of local government. The evaluation of these courses by the Youth and Community Officer revealed a high demand for them to be repeated.

The steering committee thus began to realise that joint training is a key to successful inter-agency co-operation; that only when they have learnt to co-operate will agencies be able to motivate the community; that inter-agency training must also involve middle and senior management; and that until this takes place lack of understanding of each other's roles, philosophies and tasks may stifle progress.

The work of the Consultative Group increasingly revealed the crucial influence of planning decisions on a community's ability to control crime. As a result, the work of the group attracted the interest of the City Planning Officer who asked the steering committee for their views on proposed development plans for housing in Exeter. At a specially convened meeting the committee was presented with three housing options and asked to comment. After the discussion the Planning Officer's representatives admitted that the occasion was notable for so much time being spent in considering the wider social impact of planning. Minutes of the discussion were submitted to the Council Development Committee, but attracted little support or comment because of their brevity and lack of clear recommendations.

Later another planning application was sent to the steering committee about the conversion of a building to an amusement arcade near the city shopping centre. Comments were sought on its possible effect on the environment. As a result of the previous experience, more detailed research was carried out, providing evidence which was accepted and used by the council when the conversion application was considered.*

---

* Later, in 1979, the writer gave evidence as an expert witness on behalf of the council in the Crown Court when the Amusement Company appealed against the refusal to give them a licence. His evidence was that the Amusement Arcade would bring crime into a street which hitherto had been relatively crime-free. This statement was accepted by the Judge and he refused to grant a licence. Some six months later, however, the council granted the Arcade a Gaming Licence.

The steering committee was well aware of its limitations in developing an advisory role and individual members realised that if they wanted to influence a council decision then they must learn to communicate information in a form acceptable to local politicians. Their experience suggested that in future they must ensure the continuing co-operation and commitment of the Planning Department to claim credibility in the eyes of senior local politicians. A second matter also involved the major issue of the limits of their role in relation to that of local political organisations.

After twelve months' work members of the Consultative Group were interviewed as to the way they saw its future development. Differences of perspective became immediately clear.

The police saw it as re-establishing the Anglo-Saxon concept of policing, i.e. the responsibility of each and every citizen to police. The work of the group was countering both public assumptions that policing was the sole responsibility of the police and police assumptions that policing had little or nothing to do with anyone else, i.e. they saw it as providing a basis for collaborative practical action.

The Probation Service saw the group in a very different way, mainly as a forum for discussion and learning in which the statutory agencies would hammer out differences and exert influence on local policies.

The perspective of the Youth and Community Service was that the group could be used to acquire and share resources and this they had already demonstrated could be done in the running of holiday play schemes and intermediate treatment projects.

The planners saw its advantages as identifying new criteria to influence new planning decisions. In the past they had invariably only considered the physical elements in planning and paid scant attention to its social impact. More importance had been placed on the proposed building's elevation, the colour of tiles or its height etc. than its social implications.

Two agencies viewed the police initiative with some suspicion. First there were those in the social services who saw dangers in the police stepping outside its traditional role and invading *their* territory. A number of them seemed to want to preserve a negative image of the police, in particular to emphasise its role in social control. This perspective allowed them to justify their refusal to work with the police. However, the police insistence on combining order and care divided social workers, many of them wanting to work with the police in their new role.

Certain councillors also had reservations about the project from its inception. What worried them was the strength of representation on the group. If the police managed to marshal it to speak with a collective voice, this might lead to a direct challenge to their powers. The incident of the Leisure Centre (page 24, chapter 2) had frightened some. The very nature of the police information on this issue had dictated what the decision should be. Thus, when the ruling party went against police advice, they were attacked by the opposition as building crime into society and this was also seen as direct encouragement to the people living in the proposed area to protest against the project. Therefore, they thought it essential for the group to use local authority procedures to communicate with local politicians, otherwise they would withdraw their support.

Each agency thus had its own distinct perspective of the Consultative Group though each admitted being broadly in agreement with its aims. However, as the chairman said, though the concept was correct in theory it was difficult to apply in practice. The difficulties were identified as follows:

(a) There were entrenched views amongst and between agencies, the most serious being the lack of trust.

(b) The different organisational structures, philosophies and language produced conflict.

(c) Agencies responded at different speeds to a specific problem.

(d) Those outside local government were ignorant of the latter's bureaucratic system.

(e) Some of the local government representatives had fears of damaging their personal reputations and promotion prospects vis-à-vis their political masters. These fears inhibited their action and commitment.

(f) There were already distinct signs that local politicians would only use the group when it was to their advantage.

(g) It was apparent that many of the representatives did not like to be associated with 'policing'.

(h) There were already signs of high turnover in the group membership due to promotion and transfers.

Reflecting on these difficulties the group agreed that the best ways to overcome these were through inter-agency training at all levels including inter-agency placement schemes.

What was clear to the representatives were the advantages of a group of this kind.

1. The group was independent of established political structures.
2. Its membership was broadly based and very influential.
3. It had no income or executive powers, therefore agencies had to re-think their roles and priorities rather than demand further resources.
4. It promoted inter-agency co-operation and sharing of resources.
5. It was an independent forum for discussion and for sharing problems.
6. It pooled data which was effective in reducing crime and associated social problems.
7. It created awareness of the connection between bad planning (in the widest sense) and crime. (They realised that the poor use of resources or indifferent decision making in local government and other agencies led to increased crime and delinquency.)
8. It promoted interdependence.

Since the group started in 1977 it has continued to meet, the terms of reference are still operative, member agencies are still attending, and only the structure has changed. The steering committee is now defunct and the group meets as a whole every three months. At the meeting a police Inspector from the Youth Support Team usually identifies problems concerning crime or delinquency. A small working party is then formed to report back to the main body by the next meeting with recommendations as to what members could do to improve matters. In some cases radical changes in policy and practice have been achieved. For example, a small working party looked at a geographical area which was suffering from increasing juvenile delinquency. Its preliminary recommendations were that the youth leader and police constable working in the area should be moved. The police and Youth and Community Service accepted these recommendations and replaced these officers with others who had demonstrated greater ability to activate community resources more effectively in controlling youth crime and delinquency.

5. Inter-Agency Placements in Police, Probation and Social Services

The previous chapters outlined some of the difficulties encountered when pursuing objectives of co-operation and co-ordination between the different agencies in Exeter. Resentment, jealousy and suspicion were often displayed when policemen acted outside what, in the eyes of many, was their 'traditional' role. Yet those policemen enacting this role admitted that the gulf between themselves and other workers was growing wider, both at local and national levels.

The gulfs at national level were typified in 1976 when the police orchestrated a law and order campaign aimed at getting the support of the 'silent majority'. They hoped that 'if sufficient people responded to the campaign then the voice of the ordinary citizen would begin to be heard instead of being drowned in the babble of special pleading' (1). In fact, the campaign provoked tirades from senior policemen against 'namby pamby social workers' and other 'do-gooders', enthusiastically supported by the Police Federation and other hard liners. At the 1976 Police Federation Conference, for example, the chairman singled out social workers as a particular target on the grounds that some saw themselves as allies of the anti-social young hooligans in their battle with authority. The hoary old joke was told and retold of the social worker who informed a court that 'this young boy would not have such a bad record if only the police did not keep arresting him'. The press fuelled the flames with emotive headlines such as 'Social Workers Let Girl Become Prostitute'. This scenario inevitably polarised thoughts and attitudes and confirmed prejudices on both sides. In sum, both social workers and the police were harmed.

A commentary in the magazine *Social Work Today* (2) concluded that the community was also being harmed by the clash because, 'Policemen and a substantial sector of social work professions are hired by the community to cope with the same basic problem and hostility between them is hardly calculated to enhance their prospects of success'. Two leading commentators from opposite sides of the fence wrote articles in the same magazine on how they saw the problem. Kay Roberts, the then Chairman of the British Association of Social Workers, pleaded for 'conversation – not confrontation', in relationships between social worker and policeman (3). Tony Judge, editor of *Police*, the Police Federation magazine, appealed for 'real efforts by both sides to come together and increase understanding' (4).

It was in this hostile climate that the CPSU approached the Devon Probation and Social Services. They were asked whether they would permit policemen to be attached to their services for periods of observation. Behind this idea were a number of objectives. First, it was hoped that it would create a better understanding between agencies, out of which would develop mutual respect and understanding. Secondly, that the policeman would understand the differences in other agencies' philosophies, roles and hierarchies. Thirdly, that it would broaden the policeman's concepts of prevention. Fourthly, that it would help to discover common areas of thought, concern and interest. Fifthly, that it would create appreciation of the difficulties these organisations have in preventing crime and delinquency.

(A) Police-Probation Placements

The reception from the Probation Service was enthusiastic, the only reservation voiced being that the attachment should not take place in the policeman's working area. Within a month it was agreed that four policemen would be attached to probation officers in areas near their work places. It was felt that those most suitable would be mature sergeants or constables. Prior to the attachment the Probation Service insisted that they be furnished with a pen picture of each policeman, giving his family background, length of service and work experience.

Their attachments lasted five days, after which they each submitted a report on the value of the project. The following was a typical sample programme:

Introduction to and history of the Probation Service, observation of people visiting the office and subsequent interviews.

Visits to the homes of people on probation and subsequent interviews.

A visit to a prison to prepare social enquiry reports.

A visit to an alcoholic unit.

A visit to a prison hostel.

A visit to a juvenile court.

A visit to a group of prisoners' wives.

An introduction to the work of ancillary probation officers (volunteers).

An introduction to community service orders.

The four reports made it clear that the policemen considered their placements to be of benefit to both organisations, their comments showing that many of the objectives had been achieved, e.g.: 'Experience gained during this week's attachment has brought to light the fact that police officers do not appreciate the difficulties that the Probation Service encounter; one thing which did become apparent was the general lack of liaison between the police and Probation Service.'

Only one criticism was voiced and that was by a detective who had spent a whole morning in a Magistrates' Court, a task which he often performed, though usually in a different role.

The four officers agreed that these placements should be continued although there was some differences of opinion as to the rank of those who should take part. Two suggested that all police entrants should go through the experience while the others thought it was of most use to men awaiting promotion to sergeant or inspector. There was also a divergence of opinion over the length of the placements.

The reports also contained suggestions on how to build up closer relationships between the agencies. One policeman devised a new form which gave explicit information about the offender; another sought the creation of a new post of liaison officer whose job would be to be ensure that each agency would always know persons to contact. There was common agreement that their own attachments had already started to improve matters: 'I feel that an improvement in relations between our respective services was made which I hope can now be carried on in every day work'.

The Probation Service received reports from their own local officers which were complimentary to the policemen who had been attached to them, though there was an implication that they were not a 'representative sample' of the police service. Some probation officers felt that the four policemen could have been better briefed as to the objectives of the project, but all were keen to take more policemen on placement.

Senior management from both services met and exchanged reports and discussed the points made by their respective officers. During this discussion two new points emerged. First, the Probation Service were reconsidering their ruling that policemen could not be placed in their own areas. Secondly, they were considering requesting a reciprocal arrangement with the police service, described later in this chapter. After further internal discussion on whether to place policemen with their local probation officers, they announced that they were willing to leave the decision with the police.

When the next group of policemen were selected they attended their own local probation offices. After the placements a further evaluation took place in which it was found that only one policeman voiced a criticism – that he had not been allowed to sit in on an interview of a certain client or to read the subsequent social enquiry report. Enquiries showed that this was an isolated incident and had arisen because the client did not want the policeman present.

All the police reports made favourable comments about building new relationships and raising their own personal levels of understanding. One policeman achieved instant fame on his first attached day when he used his own contacts to get a job for a client on probation.

In 1977, having reviewed the initial report, the Chief Constable recommended to his Divisional Chief Superintendents that they should encourage this scheme in view of the benefits that emerged. Two reports submitted in early 1979 on the latest attachments demonstrated that the objectives of mutual respect and under-standing were still being achieved.

(i) Detective Sergeant:

Because of the objective differences of interest between the Probation and police, misunderstandings and conflicts can easily arise between us, not only at the operational level, but at the administrative level and decision making. The main cause of misunderstanding can arise from the nature of our roles in society where the police can be seen as the 'authority of law' exercising its power without compassion or discretion. Likewise the Probation and After Care Services can be misjudged as only being interested in sheltering or protecting those members of society who have violated legislation and should be punished. The only practical way of achieving a mutual understanding and respect for each other's role is to physically work in each other's role for a period, and this changes opinions more than any round the table conferences . . . I do not suggest the attachment drastically altered our professional methods, but it certainly brought about a greater respect for each other's points of view and will help us as individuals in future.

(ii) Uniformed Sergeant:

At the risk of being dogmatic, there has existed a sense of variance between the police and Probation Service in the concept that probation has provided a soft option for offenders. There is little doubt that up to and within the last decade such an attitude was widely hailed by the majority of police officers. In this more enlightened age of policing, however, and with the advent of the exchange scheme between various organisations within the criminal justice and social systems, a greater appreciation now exists of the various roles undertaken . . . It is of interest to note that the police service is not alone in striving to inculcate a sense of community involvement . . . I have attempted not to view the Probation Service through rose tinted spectacles and I consider there still exists a degree of scepticism, albeit healthy, between the police and Probation. This can only be erased by the furtherance and possible expansion of the current exchange system.

(B) Police-Social Services Placements

The approach to the Social Services was made at the same time as the approach to the Probation Service. The initial reaction from one of their senior training officers was to view the request as 'problematic'. Later he admitted that subsequent enquiries amongst the area training officers revealed a more positive attitude, with all of them displaying some optimism that they could place the policemen in their divisional teams. Within days of that news, official application was made to the Social Services for policemen to be attached to them. The optimism was short-lived as it look nearly twelve months before the scheme really got off the ground. During the time, telephone enquiries to various Social Services offices went unanswered until two senior policemen seized the opportunity to address the training officers at their annual meeting. The policemen gave details of the scheme and outlined other community initiatives. They were closely questioned about the objectives and the necessity for a closer relationship. The results of the Probation Service evaluation were revealed, and this alone seemed to win the argument. One senior social worker made a request to shelve the idea for another twelve months so that further thought could be given to it. This was not acceptable to the main body, the project was adopted, and within a month four policemen were attached to their local Social Services Department.

A typical programme was:

Introduction to staff – Divisional Director, Team Leader and Social Worker.

Observations at:

Pastoral Care Meeting – Schools
Assessment Centre
Old People's Home
Child Guidance Clinic
Children's Home
Adult Training Centre
Advice Surgery
Occupational Centre
Mental Hospital
Team Meeting

There were also visits to families with problems concerning children, the elderly and the mentally ill.

After the week's attachment, reports were submitted by the policemen who all thought the attachment had been 'personally rewarding'. They were astounded at the range and complexity of Social Services' duties, having previously thought that they were mainly concerned with children, and at times, people suffering from mental disorders. All were convinced they had developed new relationships, e.g: 'The attachment has paved the way to better inter service co-operation and understanding and in my opinion the scheme should continue.'

The reports went into detail on how the officers had been able to discuss and sometimes challenge the social workers' attitudes on confidentiality, ethics and professionalism, e.g: 'Most police officers criticise the Social Services, not least myself. Some of it is based on folklore, some on protracted periods waiting for them to arrive and the over use of the caution. The criticism is far from one-sided and many of us have witnessed the antagonistic social worker who veils herself in a cloak of professional ethics . . . The opportunity given in these attachments lays to rest many of the misconceptions . . .'

Realisation came that social workers and police had certain objectives in common, e.g.: 'that the function of the social worker and constable are in many ways analogous. Both of us seek a well adhered state of society without crime or undue suffering.'

The contents of these reports made such an impact that local police commanders, without recourse to Headquarters, went ahead and made further arrangements for attachments; and these have continued on a regular basis.

The social service workers have been equally enthusiastic about the success of the scheme and one extolled its advantages in the magazine *Community Care* (5). This worker saw it as overcoming myths through improved levels of face-to-face communication. One major problem overcome was that of the stereotype that each held of the other. The policemen found out that not all social workers were 'long haired, be-jeaned, anti-establishment do-gooders', whilst the social workers saw that many policemen were not 'right-wing fascist pigs'.

(C) Reciprocal Placements

The initial placement of policemen with other agencies brought about demands for reciprocal arrangements within the police service. Both the social workers and the probation officers wanted to witness police in action at first hand. With tongue in cheek, the police suggested that the workers wore uniform during the placements so that they would really share the pressures of their work. Needless to say, this offer was not taken up. Because of the structured hierarchy of the police, it was a fairly simple task to implement the scheme, each police area being required to compile and to submit a programme to Police Headquarters for approval. This procedure enabled each to compile its own particular programme, taking into consideration their local resources. The vetting at Headquarters ensured that the programme was directed towards experiencing/observing practical police work. To give an air of realism to the attachment, the hours of observing were irregular, involving both day and night duty. The following was a typical programme:

First day:
  Discussion with the senior police officers of the area on extent of territory and resources at their disposal.
  Tour of station.
  Examine communication centre in operation.
  Visit television unit.
  Examine procedures in respect of juvenile liaison.

Second day:
  Visit to CID.
  Visit to burglary squad; observe the Scenes of Crime Unit in operation and sit in on interview with victim.
  Participation in the execution of a search warrant for dangerous drugs.
  Patrol with the Licensing Squad visiting pubs and nightclubs.

Third day:
  Patrol with local community constable.
  Visit educational establishment with schools liaison policeman.
  Sit in on senior officers' policy meeting.

Fourth day:
   Duties with policeman dealing with sudden deaths and visit to local mortuary.
   Night observation in emergency car.

Fifth day:
   Charge office/cell block – observe interviews and charging of shoplifters.
   Observe policing of football match.
   Observation in panda and on traffic patrol.

The overall reaction to the week's attachment was favourable, one probation officer becoming so involved that he gave up his leave day to extend his period of attachment. In fact, he showed such intense interest that policemen had difficulty in getting him to go home. On two nights when he was supposed to finish at midnight and 10.00 p.m. he stayed until the early hours of the morning. During that week he had helped to deal with two rather spectacular suicides, after which he confessed that it was the first time he had seen a dead body, let alone visit a mortuary. Other incidents which he had attended involved fire-arms, a serious road traffic accident and several burglaries, and he also had been out with a team of policemen who specialised in dealing with football hooliganism.

Only one worker sought any change. She wanted less time examining administrative structures and more time observing situations in which the police and public came face to face. She had spent the first part of her week at her local police station, which was in a small rural town during one of its quiet periods. However, during the second part of the week she had been attached to a nearby city police headquarters and had observed a much higher level of police/public interaction.

Several expressed the view that the period of attachment should be lengthened to at least a fortnight. They all saw it as giving them an insight into how policemen worked and the pressures that were exerted upon them.

This pilot placement with the police led to a regular pattern of social workers and probation workers as observers. These attachments strengthened the working relationships between the police and the other two agencies. Such were the numbers that in some areas waiting lists quickly built up of workers seeking placement. In one area the senior policeman was gently reminded by his local Divisional Director of Social Services to increase the momentum because no one had been attached to the local Police Division for at least three months, and he had seven workers eager to be placed. He wanted the exchange of workers between Social Services and the police to be extended as part of the staff induction courses, since this would provide the best possible platform on which to construct future liaison and understanding. He argued that time spent in regular structured face to face contact was a sound investment, even in purely economic terms, and emphasised that time-consuming misunderstandings which often escalated out of all proportion to their origins could usually be avoided by these exchanges. Preconceptions on both sides about roles, spheres of activity and expectations often fell away at an early stage, to be replaced by more realistic mutual concepts and contacts.

(D) Conclusions

In general, all workers who had the experience of a placement became ambassadors for the host agency. Their experiences were told and retold in the canteen, on training courses and in other work situations. This helped to change the deep-rooted prejudices which were held by the many members of their own peer work groups, and released many of the sources of frustrations with other agencies.

How did all this occur? Simply that social and probation workers had come face to face with the harsh reality of crime. They had spoken to the victims in their time of crisis, witnessing their fear, anger, injury and shock. For some workers it was a first experience, and they started to understand why policemen almost invariably identified themselves with the victims. Perhaps they even started to feel anger or a desire for revenge when they saw at first hand the effect that a criminal act can have on an innocent person. In short, they began to focus on the victims rather than on the offenders.

They also witnessed how different the police organisation was to their own. They found a semi-military style of rank structure which separated its members into a pyramid hierarchy with emphasis on the giving and carrying out of orders. There was a pervading influence of a strict discipline code and the constant threat of being investigated. Yet they also found that policemen exercised their duties as *individual* officers of the Crown, often using their discretion by giving warnings instead of always implementing the full weight of the judicial system.

Similarly, the policeman on his replacement had probed far beyond the normal parameters of his role by delving into the life history of offenders and by having to seek solutions. Probably for the first time in his work life he saw that there were no instant solutions. In fact, he realised that his usual solution of arrest and imprisonment did not solve anything other than the immediate crisis into which he had been drawn. He saw that police decisions were in the main simple and instantaneous. The law in many ways dictated the course of events according to a policeman's interpretation. His own solution was often made in terms of simple alternatives, whereas social or probation workers were faced with a long list of alternatives, none of which were likely in the long term or short term to be complete solutions. They worked with their clients over a period of time, hoping to ease their burden so that they could become useful people in society.

As a result of his shared experience, the policeman therefore increasingly began to see the offender or his family as victims of the environment. What could you do for a battered mother with seven children living in a slum under the threat of eviction with her drunken husband constantly taking the rent money for his own pleasure? Could one influence their environment so that the cycle of disadvantage be broken, enabling the seven children to grow into responsible adulthood? In such ways the policemen perceived that the decisions of the social worker could have permanent effect on people's lives.

The policeman also saw how loosely structured the other organisations were compared with his own. A lack of discipline, but more consultation; a lack of hierarchy, but more equal status. These differences could lead to misunderstandings and conflicts between agency workers unless witnessed at first hand. What was also discovered was the common trait which linked the three agencies, that all were interested in preventing crime and in ensuring care and order. The methods of attaining these objectives were different, but in some ways complementary within each agency. It was realisations of this kind that started to create a healthy climate in which the concepts of co-operation and co-ordination could grow. It ensured that local projects such as inter-agency training, sharing of data, and joint action teams were undertaken in a spirit of mutual respect and understanding. Without these the projects would have foundered.

6. Analysis of Questionnaire Results

Consultation between police, other agencies and communities made it clear that the main themes of general concern were:

1. The police role, which included its preventive and reactive functions.
2. The role of statutory agencies in relation to preventive policing.
3. The use of data in relation to preventive policing.

These themes were explored more fully by means of a questionnaire sent to:

21 Community volunteers
17 Workers in statutory agencies
 8 City centre constables
 8 Resident constables
16 Senior police officers
   (Results are set out in tabular form in Appendix C)

1. The Police Role

The CPSU projects suggested that, in general, people supported the police developing a preventive role. However, specific preventive projects provoked different reactions. There was agreement about policemen being involved in neighbourhoods, but some alarm about policemen becoming over-involved at a time when the police service was already stretched through lack of manpower and other resources. There were also fears that such involvement demeaned their professional status. Other opposition came from policemen who wanted a narrow law enforcement role. Moreover, it was obvious from the public meeting that there was a great deal of support for reactive policing (i.e. repeated calls for more police, more powers and harsher punishments).

Was this an accurate summary? To find out, the respondents were given eight suggestions upon which they were asked to express their strength of agreement or disagreement. These suggestions involved possible reactive and preventive policies that could be implemented to curb increased delinquency. Four suggestions were reactive, four preventive. The scoring was:

Strongly disagree	1
Mildly disagree	2
Uncertain	3
Mildly agree	4
Strongly agree	5

All with the exception of the agency workers supported to some degree the overall concept of reactive policing (Table 1a.) But even they agreed with the notion of having mobile groups of policemen to contain delinquency, although this was not supported by the resident policemen. With the exception of agency workers, all respondents believed that increased numbers of policemen can contain delinquency. Neither the agency workers nor senior police officers wanted the police to divert more resources to catching young people. The city centre policemen and community volunteers wanted the police to have more powers, although this was opposed by the agency workers. The two other police groups expressed uncertainty about the need for this extra authority.

With the exception of the city centre policemen the respondents firmly agreed with the concept of preventive policing, particularly police/agency partnership (Table 1b.) All agreed with the need to increase the number of foot patrols and police/neighbourhood involvement, though the city centre and resident policemen did not think that policemen should be encouraged to create activities for young people.

The respondents made seventeen reactive and sixty-three preventive proposals on how they would contain delinquency.

With the sole exception of the agency workers, all respondents made reactive proposals involving demands for tougher punishments, increased detection rate, powers and resources (Table 2.) The following proposals were typical:

'The parents of delinquents should be made more responsible for their children's acts by heavy punishment.' (City centre constable)

'Lack of parental interest in their delinquent children could be corrected by the judiciary.' (Community volunteer)

'Plain clothes patrols are needed so as to catch potential trouble makers more easily.' (Community volunteer)

'Youngsters should be interviewed without parents present.' (City centre constable)

'Increasing the number of policemen can cure delinquency.' (Superintendent)

All the respondents emphasised the need for preventive police patrols, which they saw as best accomplished by the policeman walking his beat:

'We must transfer more men from cars to foot patrols and analyse our problems so that we patrol to prevent anticipated trends instead of patrolling afterwards.' (Chief Superintendent)

'Foot patrols strike up relationships and identify at a much earlier stage potential trouble-makers.' (Resident constable)

'We want more policemen and *policewomen* (respondent's underlining) walking around our estates. The policewomen can make a great contribution as our women folk end up with all the problems.' (Community volunteer)

Contrary to their earlier support for mobile groups of policemen, two agency workers wrote:

'Policemen must not work in groups; this causes concern and anti-establishment feeling.'

Several community volunteers expressed the belief that local policemen should be encouraged to use their discretion to caution young people, instead of resorting to a legalistic approach. Most of all, the respondents wanted the police to be involved in the community so as to ensure co-operation and mutual support:

'The police must aim at close police/public relationship and must penetrate all community institutions.' (Agency worker)

'The police should help parents to educate potential delinquents in social conscience and give them more outlets for their energies and enthusiasm.' (City centre constable)

The community volunteers suggested that the police should get involved in schools, youth clubs, play-groups and neighbourhood meetings. The school was singled out for special mention as the place where the police could do their most constructive work. They were convinced that this type of involvement was beneficial because it could help the young become socially responsible in their communities.

One respondent reminded the police that they were often seen as outsiders when, in fact, their historical roots were in the community:

'Policemen, if they are to be successful, must aim at being accepted as members of the general public by the general public.' (Community volunteer)

Only the agency workers failed to mention that other statutory agencies' policies could affect delinquency, e.g. school discipline. The resident policemen criticised local authorities for having failed to create community dialogue, or to encourage self-help:

'There must be an improvement in the liaison between local authority and the community so people feel they have a say in the control of their activities and that they get what they want.' (Resident constable)

'Agencies push facilities or amenities at people which are not wanted or sought for. Better if they became consultants and provided money so that the community could create its own activities such as its own youth clubs.' (Resident constable)

'Other agencies should do their bit to prevent juvenile delinquency by providing more resources in the places of need'. (Community volunteer)

Lastly, the senior and resident policemen, with the support of the agency workers made mention of the need for statutory agency/police partnership. They suggested that there was a need to develop joint projects such as play or leisure facilities. An alternative was a more orthodox approach through the creation of joint agency intermediate centres where young people would receive help and guidance from social workers and policemen. Some stressed that a joint agency team would be able to speak with far more authority than any single agency, particularly if it approached the community to activate self-help. A senior officer thought that the other statutory agencies would be able to share police credibility which would be to their advantage, but he also warned of the dangers of co-optation, e.g. loss of professional identity:

> 'Close co-operation with other agencies is a very desirable attitude but the police service must not run the risk of being relegated to mere membership of the group or committee. It must exercise firm control of the overall scene because the police have credibility in law enforcement. It is not presumptuous to suggest greater credibility than any other statutory agency enjoys at the present time. The public expect and respond to an element of police leadership. We are the best ones to preach a liberal doctrine. Furthermore, it is only the police that adequately understand the problem of victims.' (Chief Superintendent)

The respondents were then given the opportunity of suggesting how they wanted crime areas to be policed. First, they arranged six reactive and preventive proposals into a priority order, and next gave their own suggestions (Tables 3 and 4).

The *agency workers* preferred prevention by tighter environmental control – such as bringing transport times into line with licensing hours and implementing technical crime prevention. However, they still placed some importance on the need for a uniformed presence. They gave lowest priority to the three reactive suggestions.

The *city centre constables* gave first priority to the reactive proposal to increase the number of policemen in the area. Then they selected two preventive proposals – seeking tighter environmental control and a continued uniform 'presence' on the ground. Their responses appeared to be balanced between reactive and preventive proposals. This was probably the result of the empirical data revealing, for example, that some crime areas were formed as people walked home after public transport had stopped.

The *community volunteers* supported both reactive and preventive proposals. They wanted tight environmental control and patrols by plain clothes officers. However, they did not like the idea that the level of policing in crime areas should be increased at the expense of denuding other parts of the city.

Likewise, the *resident constables* supported a mix of reaction and prevention in crime areas. They wanted increased numbers of policemen and patrols by plain clothes officers to counteract the problem but at the same time they accepted the need for environmental control.

The *senior officers* gave priority to both reactive and preventive policing proposals. Although their first priority was reactive, it entailed going to the magistrates and asking them to cut back the licensing hours. Their next priority was to pursue improvements in environmental control and to implement crime prevention surveys.

Overall there was a bias towards prevention, but there was a low numerical response from the police and community groups, which made it difficult to draw any conclusions from their suggestions. However, what was significant was the firm minority response from the agency workers who wanted the police to introduce a reactive approach by implementing strict police supervision of night clubs and public houses, and the demand for increased penalties for infringement of the licensing laws:

'This will ensure that the licensees comply with them.'

This demand was undoubtedly brought about by the empirical data which showed that the locations of specific categories of crime invariably clustered around such premises. It also prompted similar comments from the senior officers and community volunteers:

'They attract them in with their bright lights and drinks, then chuck them out in the early hours of the morning. It's an invitation to mob violence. We should cut back their hours.' (Community volunteer)

'Magistrates must inflict greater penalties on licensees of club premises where breaches of licensing laws are detected, in particular, under-age drinking and supplying drunken persons.' (Chief Superintendent)

One community volunteer suggested that the solution lay in the police carrying out aggressive patrolling:

'Armed policemen and dog patrols should be outside all the night clubs at chucking out time – that will keep them in order and make the honest citizen feel safer.'

All the groups suggested solutions which involved some form of environmental control – this again was prompted by empirical data which had revealed that one crime area was poorly lighted and the fact that the planners were considering an application for a night club to open in a non-crime area:

'The city authority should do some forward planning. Put the night clubs close together so that we can keep an eye on them. Put them away from residential areas so that we don't get the complaints.' (Resident constable)

The community and agency respondents also wanted the community to be informed so that it could accept some measure of responsibility:

'Community associations must find ways to provide alternative interests where alcoholic drinks are not the magnet. Where school leavers can find interesting occupations for self-development.' (Community volunteer)

'By gaining the co-operation of the persons responsible for clubs and pubs you will make them aware of their need to provide proper supervision.' (Agency worker)

One resident constable criticised policemen who patrolled in cars; he saw this as a possible encouragement to anti-social behaviour:

'It is only the uniform presence on foot that has any deterrent effect. Cruising panda cars makes it all a game to the yob.'

In relation to the police role in 'juveniles at risk' areas, the empirical data was shown to the respondents, showing in what neighbourhoods there were increasing, constant or decreasing numbers of juvenile offenders. It also showed that young people in neighbourhoods with delinquency problems had the least access to youth amenities. The respondents were then asked a number of questions in order to obtain their views on what the police should do in such areas (Table 5).

Most respondents were wholly in agreement with the notion that the police should involve themselves in the total problem of juvenile delinquency, but a substantial minority amongst the community volunteers and constables thought not, on the grounds that the police already had enough to do!

'Extra duties should only be taken on by the police if they have increased resources.' (Community volunteer)

'Involvement is not good because future contacts in that area will obviously be reactive and also present workloads do not give us a chance to get more involved.' (Resident constable)

'There appears to be more than enough organisation to deal with this aspect and too few policemen to detect crime. We can't cope with the increase of crime let alone anything else.' (City centre constable)

How then did they want 'juveniles at risk' areas to be policed? To answer this they placed six reactive and preventive proposals in the order that they would want them implemented (Table 6).

These responses showed a high degree of agreement on how the area should be policed. All thought that the most important priority in areas of high delinquency was for the police to approach other statutory agencies to set up inter-agency action groups. The second most important priority was for the police to involve local people in dealing with the problem. The third priority was the acceptance that the level of uniformed policemen on foot patrol should be increased in these areas. Clearly there was complete agreement that the overall approach by the police to areas of high delinquency should be through the implementation of preventive techniques, and there was also a great deal of agreement on the order of priority for the specific preventive proposals.

The respondents' views on preventive and reactive aspects of the police role were as follows:

Agency workers
1. Initially they expressed uncertainty about the concepts of reactive policing, with specific disapproval of proposals for increased police powers. There was some support for mobile groups of policemen, although within their own groups there were

those who specifically warned against it. They expressed some support for preventive policing, particularly with agency and community involvement. Their own proposals to combat delinquency were preventive – police/agency partnership; police/neighbourhood support; and the re-introduction of uniformed foot patrols.

2. In crime areas they favoured a preventive police strategy with police involvement in communities. However, some also recognised the need for reactive strategies, particularly in the control and sale of alcohol.

3. In the 'juveniles at risk' areas, all believed that the police should involve themselves in the problems of delinquency beyond arresting offenders. They wanted a police role based on prevention, police/agency partnership, police/neighbourhood involvement, and increased numbers of uniformed police on foot patrol.

Community volunteers

1. They expressed firm support for all aspects of reactive policing, particularly the concentration of more resources into catching young people and increasing the numbers of policemen. At the same time, they also expressed firm support for preventive policing, particularly police/neighbourhood support and foot patrols. In fact, their own proposals were overwhelmingly preventive: they suggested police/community involvement, foot patrols, and that there should be improvements in the social policies of other agencies. The small minority of reactive proposals were for tougher punishments and means to increase detection rate.

2. In crime areas this group favoured both reactive *and* preventive policing strategies, particularly those entailing environmental control and patrols by policemen in plain clothes.

3. Most believed the police should involve themselves in the whole problem of delinquency, especially in 'juveniles at risk' areas. They wanted the police to be preventive biased –police/neighbourhood involvement and police/agency partnership.

Resident constables

1. They expressed support for reactive policing, particularly for increasing the number of policemen. They were uncertain about the need for increased police powers and for mobile groups of policemen. Like the community respondents they firmly supported preventive policing, particularly neighbourhood involvement and foot patrols. They were uncertain about encouraging policemen to set up activities for young people, but their own proposals were overwhelmingly preventive with emphasis on the value of foot patrols and the need for improvements in the social policies of other agencies; only a small minority sought tougher punishments and an increase in the detection rate.

2. In crime areas this group wanted reactive *and* preventive police strategies, in particular an increase in the numbers of uniformed and plain clothes policemen; and also higher levels of environmental control.

3. In 'juveniles at risk' areas most of the residential constables thought the police should involve themselves in the whole problem of delinquency. They wanted the police role based on prevention – police/agency partnerships; an increase in the numbers of uniformed policemen on foot patrol; and police/ neighbourhood involvement.

City centre constables

1. They supported reactive policing, particularly the suggestion that the police should concentrate more resources into detecting young people and setting up mobile patrols. They were uncertain about preventive policing, although they firmly supported increasing the number of foot patrols. They were against encouraging policemen to set up activities for young people, and their own proposals were almost evenly split between reaction and prevention. They wanted tougher punishments and means to achieve increased detection rates, police powers and resources. However, they accepted the need for police/community involvement, preventive patrolling and that other agencies should improve their social policies.

2. This group favoured reactive *and* preventive police strategies

in crime areas, particularly increasing the levels of manpower and environmental control.

3. Most of them believed that the police should involve themselves in the whole problem of delinquency. They wanted a police role based on preventive policies in areas of high delinquency; police/agency partnership; an increase in the numbers of uniformed policemen; and police/neighbourhood involvement.

Senior officers

1. They were lukewarm about reactive policing, though they favoured mobile groups of policemen and an increase in police numbers. However, they were uncertain about the need for more police powers and any further concentration of resources into detection. The were firmly in agreement with preventive policing, particularly police/neighbourhood involvement and police/agency partnership. Their own proposals were two-thirds preventive and one-third reactive. They emphasised the importance of police involvement with the community, preventive patrolling, agency partnership, and the need for other agencies to improve their social policies. Their reactive proposals were for means to achieve increased detection rates, more police resources, and tougher punishments.

2. In crime areas this group favoured both preventive *and* reactive police strategies. They wanted environmental control e.g. on night clubs, opening hours, and bus timetables.

3. All of them thought that the police should involve themselves in the whole problem of delinquency. In areas of high delinquency they wanted a police role which was based on prevention – police/agency partnership; police/neighbourhood involvement; and an increase in the numbers of uniformed policemen on foot patrols.

Conclusions

Overall there was an awareness of the limitations of formal or statutory control systems in society, and that both preventive and reactive policing have limitations. The two concepts of policing were seen as complementary, but if employed alone, could produce dysfunctions. Perhaps most significant was the agreement that different localities and different problems required different styles of policing.

2. The Role of Statutory Agencies and Voluntary Organisations in Preventive Policing

It will be recalled that many of the CPSU projects involved other statutory agencies, based on the beliefs that other agencies and voluntary organisations probably had greater effect on crime and delinquency than the police, and that their influence could be all the greater within a co-ordinated approach. This belief was supported by many of the key personnel who were interviewed, although some policemen had their doubts. It was therefore of prime value to obtain the respondents' views on how they saw the role of the statutory agencies in preventive policing.

The respondents were first asked to consider a list of eleven agencies and organisations (from which the police were omitted), and to indicate those which could best remedy the problems of areas of high delinquency (Table 7).

The total number of agencies/organisations seen as being able to help varied from group to group. More than half the *agency workers* suggested that all eleven could help in some way. *All* of them identified the Social Services and the Youth and Community Services as the most influential.

Community volunteers suggested that only four out of the eleven could help. Over three-quarters of them emphasised the influence of the Youth and Community Service and Neighbourhood Associations.

Resident constables selected ten, only omitting the Health Service. *All* of them identified the Youth and Community Service, Schools, Neighbourhood Associations and Councillors as being most influential in combatting problems of juvenile delinquency.

The *city centre constables* suggested six out of the eleven, identifying the Youth and Community Service and Housing Department as the ones who could have the most effect. One city centre constable cynically commented:

> 'They showed no interest or action in the past. The only person who does show interest is the victim.'

Lastly, the *senior officers* selected eight out of the eleven, and like the community respondents, identified the Youth and Community Service and the Neighbourhood Associations as being most influential.

The selected agencies which were common to all five groups were:
Social Services; Youth and Community Service; Schools; and Neighbourhood Associations.

Except for the resident constables, all of them suggested a number of other organisations that could assist, e.g. 42% of the agency workers emphasised the important influence that a play-group could have on an area whilst the city centre policemen stressed the importance of involving the press, public, and uniformed youth organisations such as the cadet corps.

The group next went on to suggest ways in which these agencies could give assistance (Table 8).

With the exception of the community volunteers and the city centre constables, all respondents agreed that the main contribution would be for agencies to co-ordinate their approaches to local problems:

> 'These high delinquent areas are joint problems which cannot be handled by the police alone.' (Agency worker)

> 'It has to be a combined effort to solve this problem.' (Resident constable)

> 'Professional barriers lead to professional incompetence. There must be co-ordination between all these agencies.' (Superintendent)

The community volunteers put their main faith in relevant data for more effective decision making:

> 'It must be of use to the planner.'

Several community volunteers also emphasised the need for a joint approach, themselves included:

> 'Prevention is better than cure and awareness reduces risk. With this knowledge *we* can all plan *together* for the future.'

> 'We must seek to deal with the situation within the community. It's *our* problem.'

The city centre constables, however, insisted that the greatest contribution these agencies could make would be to improve the quality and sum total of facilities in these target areas, e.g. schools opening after hours and uniformed youth organisations being encouraged or even subsidised to open in such areas.

'These areas need facilities for exciting play.' (City centre constable)

Conclusions
The respondents agreed:-

(a) That policing, in Alderson's definition, is a function of most agencies and organisations (that is, as long as this country wishes to continue the traditional system of policing with the consent and co-operation of the citizens).
(b) That many of the problems facing society are common and demand joint action.
(c) That there must be a redistribution of resources which can only come about by joint consultation and mutual aid.

3. The Use of Data for Preventive Policing
The CPSU policemen had used empirical crime data to get people to respond to a preventive policing initiative. There was a demand for their data, particularly from agency workers and people in the community. When it was released, people reacted in a variety of ways, e.g. by developing community projects; by raising their level of co-operation with other statutory agencies; or by just feeling more secure in their localities.

Yet not all viewed the data in such a positive way. Others, especially those working in the statutory agencies, expressed misgivings about the release of data, being concerned (a) about breaches of confidentiality and/or (b) that the data would be misused, thereby stigmatising or causing alarm. Certain policemen went as far as to dismiss the data as useless.

The respondents were therefore shown visual examples of empirical crime data in order to find out their responses to it. Crime and juvenile risk areas were explained by showing the different patterns of crime in a city, many of which seemed to be the product of poor policies or facilities, e.g. 'dumping' policies of the Housing Department or lack of transport.

The respondents then considered whether data on 'juveniles at risk' areas was of use to them (Table 9). Police responses were combined since there was little or no difference between the views of the various police groups.

All the agency workers indicated that delinquency data was of use · to them. However, one did express some concern: 'This information is useful to me in my job, but public knowledge could create worry in the community.'

Only a very small minority of community and police respondents expressed uncertainty (9% and 3% respectively): and another small minority among the same respondents (9% and 9%) dissented. The police dissenters pursued two lines of arguments: that research was not needed as the facts were already known; and that the police should concentrate on surveillance of known target criminals.

'One should study and know the criminals and not the area.' (Superintendent)

'We all know that the majority of juvenile offenders live on council estates.' (City centre constable)

Overall, however, the great majority emphasised that they could use the data.

The respondents then chose ways in which they would use the data (Table 10).

The community volunteers were adamant that they could take action themselves:

'*My* community association can make a contribution to alleviate the problem.'

'If *I* thought of running a youth club in such an area, would that help to improve things?'

'*We* can create interest for young people if *we* know the extent of the problem.'

The agency workers thought their personal work performance would improve from this increased knowledge:

'I need to know this when dealing with my clients. It helps to change my perspectives of them.'

'This is essential background knowledge to social problems in the city.'

Similar remarks were made by some of the police respondents:

It's nice to know what I'm walking into, at least I'll understand their problem a bit better.' (Resident constable)

'This does give me an overall picture of my city as my own view is blinkered by my own personal experiences which are limited to eight hours a day 5 days a week.' (City centre constable)

Probably the most poignant remark about the use of data was:

'Once stigmatised an area keeps a reputation. We who live in those areas are *anxious* to know the facts.' (Community volunteer)

This *cri de coeur* was made by a person who has lived in a neighbourhood which has been stigmatised since the day it was built over fifty years ago. Other respondents saw the knowledge simply in terms of increased understanding:

'It is reassuring to know the official picture.'

'It helps me to understand what is really going on and why.'

Most policemen suggested that they would use the data to pursue co-operation with other statutory and voluntary organisations:

'This information does indicate why we must involve agencies and communities.' (Chief Superintendent)

'This method of visual analysis is now used in my division and has given me a new positive attitude to the way in which policing should be carried out.' (Superintendent)

'With this sort of information you can go to schools, parents, social services and others to demand joint action.' (City centre constable)

Some community volunteers also saw the data as providing the means by which they could achieve co-operation with certain statutory agencies. From their comments it was obvious that they viewed some of these agencies' social policies as contributing to the problems of 'juveniles at risk' area.

> 'This will help us to insist that they spread problem families around instead of concentrating them on one estate.' (Community volunteer)

Half of the police suggestions for the use of data (Table 11) concerned preventive proposals in the planning and deployment of their resources, e.g. 'A policeman on foot, even if he only showed a uniform in such an area, would be a deterrent.' A third of their proposals were indecisive in direction, e.g. 'If I had them I would put more policemen into the area.' Only a very small minority (10%) favoured a mixed response of reaction and prevention; and an even smaller group favoured pure reaction: 'A task force would soon sort them out.'

Most of the respondents thought that the police should release information on 'juveniles at risk' areas. However, a very small minority amongst police and community dissented (9% and 5% respectively). The community volunteer thought that the data should be kept for police use only whilst the police dissenters argued that it would be a wasted effort to release such information:

> 'It's a waste of time telling other agencies. They don't do anything except close their eyes. Although the Neighbourhood Associations may be of some use.' (City centre constable)

Conclusions

The respondents were in general agreement about the role that data can play in preventive policing, and their views correlated with the experience of the CPSU

(a) That empirical crime data is of use, and should be released.
(b) That this release can lead to improved decision making; to increased co-operation; to more effective action, and to greater understanding.

7. Analysis of Group Discussions

The final stage of the research was to obtain the views of the various groups on three main issues.

1. The priorities of the police.
2. Relationships between police and other agencies and organisations.
3. Relationships between police and community.

In their discussions each group considered:

(a) The advantages and disadvantages of reactive and preventive policing.
(b) Difficulties of implementing CPSU proposals at a practical level.

1. The Priorities of the Police

Discussion amongst the senior officers and city centre constables initially centred around a demand for reactive policies. They wanted specialist squads, increased detection rates and quicker response times to emergencies in order to deal with public disorder, traffic and crime. They were certain that greater emphasis on reaction would reduce crime:

> The most effective preventive measure would be a 100% detection rate. The certainty of getting caught prevents crime. No matter what the punishment is afterwards – if they're going to get caught they will think twice about it. So, obviously, as a result of that we have to concentrate on catching the offenders committing crime.' (City centre constable)

This emphasis was supported, to some degree, by the agency workers who saw organised crime requiring reactive policies – inevitably demanding large-scale police resources, whilst 'mass' crime demanded a quite different approach. The problem, as they saw it, was 'finding the balance'.

Significantly, most groups saw mass (i.e. petty or opportunist) crime as more personally threatening than organised crime. The latter was something they read about in the newspapers or saw on television, whilst petty crime was something which they had direct knowledge of, and which threatened their personal sense of security. They saw opportunist crime as being preventable since it was largely the product of inadequate environmental planning; lack of social awareness; poor education; lack of parental involvement with children etc. And all thought that it was in this area that the police lacked both policies and expertise.

The city centre constables, for example, were critical of the whole criminal justice system. They complained that the judiciary, social and probation services were 'sat back waiting for business', and were only active after problems had erupted. As their criticisms developed so they realised that the police service was in a similar position and that their own obsession with reaction had been at the expense of developing preventive policies and expertise:

> 'I think we have a part to play even beforehand. I don't think it is entirely a police matter. The whole point of being a policeman is obviously to protect life and property and prevent crime. That's before detection, but we don't do too much to it at the present time because there is so much crime to detect and so many offenders to punish. As my colleagues say, I think there must be a lot less emphasis on what happens after these people have turned into offenders and a lot more emphasis based on what happens before, so that hopefully, we get a decrease in crime because of the different social awareness.' (City centre constable)

This theme was picked up by the agency workers who were sceptical about the emphasis being placed by the police on prevention. They only saw a few policemen attempting to implement preventive procedures whilst the majority were mainly engaged in reactive practices. What they wanted was a balance of effort, although they were doubtful as to how this could be achieved. They expected a quick response to emergencies as well as policemen walking the beat. The police groups also agreed that a preventive strategy should be developed, but were uncertain how this could be achieved.

The senior officers thought lack of manpower was a main factor, e.g:

'You don't know where to get the bobbies from to prevent what's going on, and we lose this battle every year and so is the country losing the same battle.'

'The police strength has got to be more realistic.'

' . . . has got the stabbings. I doubt he's got a spare man in the Division. . . . so and so has just got a murder and it took a hell of a lot of men on that enquiry . . . We haven't got the luxury of doing anything preventive even in the winter because we are sort of scraping the bones all the time for manpower.'

The city centre constables, however, accused their senior officers of wasting manpower and other resources because of their obsession with technology and specialisation:

'When you're sitting about in the station you're not preventing crime. You're not protecting people. Yet, in the City Centre, more than half of the establishment is inside the station. Collators, radio operators, computer operators, the process office, gaolers and so on – more than half are in the station.' (City centre constable)

A number of solutions were suggested involving a redevelopment of manpower and a revaluation of priorities. The suggestion of one senior officer was to 'push policemen out of the offices at peak periods'. Another deployed his men away from traffic duties.

One constable advocated the withdrawal of 'panda' cars because the public would be better served by a three tier system: the first tier being policemen patrolling on foot; the second tier, that of a double crewed emergency car; the third tier, that of experienced police staff at Headquarters who could provide specialist services, and more importantly, could evaluate the calls upon the police services so as to make appropriate responses in terms of manpower.

All agreed that the essential reason for a preventive strategy was to ensure the retention of public sympathy and public cooperation.

'Our main priority must be prevention. I think it will be a sad day if we get around to the other side of it. Because the public will undoubtedly suffer. They will be the losers in the long run because we will not be so effective.' (City centre constable)

Thus, for the police to be effective, they have to create a sense of security and stability in individual citizens as well as in the community as a whole. All agreed that this could only be accomplished by the reinstatement of the uniformed policeman on foot patrol. As one community volunteer said, 'The police gave up preventing crime when they put a policeman in a car'. However, the agency workers and community volunteers wanted more than mere police presence; they wanted policemen to identify with their communities:

> 'I think the idea of having a copper on the beat is nice. It gives a sense of security. But it is not an effective method either in reacting or preventing unless he gets involved in local problems.' (Agency worker)

The community volunteers defined the benefits of preventive policing as follows:

(a) It was cheaper for the community to pay for a preventive rather than a reactive strategy.
(b) It would reduce total crime.
(c) The community can help policemen who implement preventive policies, but are unable to help those who carry out reactive policies.
(d) It was more fulfilling for policemen to concentrate on prevention than to deal with the consequences of crime.
(e) It improved the policeman's ability to support formal and informal control systems.

However, each group of respondents identified three main weaknesses in police organisation which needed to be remedied as a matter of urgency if policemen were to be encouraged to identify with their communities.

(i) Both the agency workers and community volunteers pointed to problems created by the police career structure and the resultant mobility of personnel (although the respondents admitted that the similar criticism could be applied to most public services, particularly the social services):

'I think one of the greater problems is that we're only in a situation for a short time, then somebody leaves and somebody new comes along. You get to know a policeman, then he is promoted and he has changed his department. We are all professional people and we all move up and up.' (Agency worker)

'We want to go back to the time when a constable who entered the force had his sole aim to be a policeman. A lot of policemen entering the force today go for a career structure; you try to attract the university entrants with the prospects of promotion. It really is a rat race. We need some of the old-fashioned chaps again in this respect. I always think of our P. C. Dave Foster. He says, "I want to be a policeman and the moment I move away from that I have lost my job satisfaction. I want to remain amongst my people." That's the man you should be encouraging.' (Community volunteer)

Several agreed that the solution lay in the police service developing a lateral career structure for policemen who had demonstrated their ability to work in neighbourhoods, to encourage them to remain at grass-roots level. Only one respondent warned of the dangers of policemen over-identifying, thus losing their integrity of purpose.

(ii) The community volunteers and police groups emphasised the problems of young policemen who displayed 'overbearing and immature personalities'. Because of this they thought young policemen often incapable of forming effective relationships with their communities. The community volunteers were scathing about such policemen, using such words as: 'Pasty-faced boys; lacking in size; lacking in authority; pale; inexperienced; abrupt; nervous; kids in uniform'. Claims were made that specific crime problems such as assaults on police or public disorder often developed as a result of this immaturity:

'I mean, you get a young policeman 20 years of age. He goes on to the beat and he goes down to the nightclubs or into town and he sees a couple of yobbos, you know, misbehaving themselves. Now, an older policemen would know how to approach these youngsters – by saying, "Cut that out, there's no need for it". Whereas a young policeman would have that attitude to stick out his chest and say, "Right now, which one is going to start it?" You see what I mean? One stops trouble, the other helps trouble. That is the difference.' (Community volunteer)

The senior officers also agreed that police/community relations sometimes suffered because of the inexperience of young policemen:

'What's the use of a couple more men on the beat if 13 weeks ago they were bank clerks? They haven't got a clue what policing is about and because of that could create the very law and order problem we are talking about. They can, at times, cause us a lot of problems.' (Chief Superintendent)

'It's nearly always the young bobbies that get assaulted. The older ones know how to handle the situation.' (Superintendent)

There was general agreement that these failures derived from a young policeman's training and the fact that he often patrolled in a panda car remote from his community:

'The fact is that we are not using them because we are putting them in cars. We are isolating them from the public. We're making sure that they only meet the public in a stress situation – then we wonder why they get into trouble.' (Chief Superintendent)

The constables also criticised police management policy which resulted in their young colleagues being put under pressure to achieve measurable results in terms of numbers of arrests and prosecutions.

A community volunteer suggested the solution lay in the inexperienced policemen starting their careers on foot in the housing estates under the guidance of local resident constables. By having to work closely with their mature colleagues it was thought that young policemen would quickly learn how to relate to and interact with the public:

'I think it would be a good idea if young policemen had to help out in the community. It would help them in their work with members of the general public. Because you will find the young policeman hasn't got the same attitude towards members of the general public as the older policeman has. I think it would help to break the policeman in on how to work with the public.' (Community volunteer)

The police groups suggested similar solutions, e.g. that it must be a matter of priority for management to improve training techniques, and 'on the job' supervision, and to ensure that trainee policemen walk the beat so that they can learn from their communities.

(iii) The final weakness identified concerned the present status and function of the uniformed policeman on the beat, which many saw as having been devalued within the police organisation. The resident constables were particularly sensitive on this score, seeing themselves relegated to the bottom of the police hierarchy:

'They, the CID and Traffic, seem to look down on us. They seem to look upon themselves as better than us. They say, "Poor chap walking around the beat". We are treated as the lowest of the low in the Police Force. We are, you know. We are seen as failures; we fail to get promotion; we fail to get into CID; when in fact the uniformed man on his feet is the actual man doing the job of controlling crime.'

'The bloke on the ground is too often devalued. I mean the emphasis by the bosses is still on specialist departments such as CID, Traffic and others.'

Again there was some measure of agreement amongst the various police groups that here was yet another failure of police management:

'We leave him (resident constable) alone simply because he is one of the link men between the police and the community. We still like him to *plod* around as a familiar face. We vary their duties a bit so that they are in the problem areas, but we haven't *bothered* to bring him into a group system of policing. I suppose we all agree it is the most essential job – the bloke in contact with his patch. We all say that this is the most essential thing, but actually, we are *giving him the lowest* of priorities.' (Chief Superintendent)

The senior officers suggested ways that might rectify this lack of status:

(a) That the resident policeman should be given 24 hour responsibility for his neighbourhood with extra salary.

(b) That constables should be graded, the top grade being Resident Constable with a title such as 'Area Officer'.

(c) That the CID and Traffic departments should consult the resident constables on matters relating to the prosecution of offenders in their areas.

Conclusions

The discussions on police priorities showed general agreement that police must develop a preventive strategy. All saw it being based upon uniformed policemen on foot, the most important benefits being (i) greater public support and co-operation; and (ii) a greater sense of security in the community.

Although recognising the value of such a strategy, there were warnings that it might not be possible to implement it because of lack of manpower. There were also major problems about the devalued status of resident constables within the organisation. This had developed because management had concentrated on developing specialised technological and reactive policies. There was, therefore, a need to change priorities, giving greater emphasis to proposals such as three-tier policing and to an increased stature for beat policemen.

2. Relationships between Police and Other Agencies and Organisations

During the various discussions a number of statutory agencies and other organisations were singled out for criticism on the grounds that they were helping to create conditions in which crime and delinquency flourished:

> 'Very often it is the policemen who are picking up the results of bad planning, bad facilities, the lack of youth clubs and all the other things.' (Agency worker)

The following were mentioned:

Supermarkets – both agency workers and community volunteers blamed the commercial policies which had led to the increase in shoplifting.

Magistrates – there was general agreement that the judiciary had failed to ensure a strict control on the sale of alcohol; and to inflict appropriate punishments on those that infringe the licensing laws.

Press and television – the agency workers were very critical of the media's portrayal of crime. The approach was either to glamourise or to sensationalise crime instead of dealing with it in an informative and objective manner.

Licensing trade – again there was general agreement about the lack of responsibility being displayed by many brewers, publicans, night-club owners and supermarkets in their sale of drink. Some of their policies were seen as hypocritical. For instance, the brewers spent colossal sums on advertising their products and then became alarmed at an increase in pub violence undoubtedly related to increased consumption.

Politicians – both the police and agency workers criticised the politicians for their failure to provide amenities in the areas of greatest need and their reluctance to consult experienced professionals.

Planners – there was general condemnation of planners' failure to consider the social environment when planning housing estates. This was seen as a major contributory cause of delinquency. Like politicians, planners were seen as all too remote and aloof from the processes of life.

Housing Department – the agency workers and community volunteers blamed the policies which seemed to be leading to a concentration of problem families in some areas.

Education – agency workers criticised the Education Department's reluctance to allow school premises to be used by the community, particularly out of term time.

Public transport – agency workers blamed some crime problems on the lack of public transport in certain areas at key times of the day.

These failures were not seen as a result of deliberate policies but rather as occurring by default, the results of a lack of communication and collaboration between agencies:

'Strangely enough, in all the bits and pieces that we have been dealing with on paper today and all we deal with in division, the local authorities are rarely involved. We get no lead or guidance from these newly formed authorities. We are not in contact with them on the reduction of crime or the reduction of public disorder. The only time we hear from local authorities is if they have a problem regarding public order when they will come to us, but they don't give us any lead.' (Chief Superintendent)

On this failure of collaboration the police constables recalled various incidents in which other statutory agencies' decisions had caused problems to local policing. One resident constable gave the example of a local authority building old peoples' flats with curved sloping thoroughfares going through the middle of the complex. He was certain that knowing the nature of the neighbourhood, he could have warned the authorities of the probable outcome if he had seen the plans beforehand. Now complaints were being received about young people skateboarding along the thorough-fares to the danger of the old folk, and the local authority had accused *him* of failing to prevent this. It was therefore generally agreed that there was a necessity for some form of co-operation to be developed.

'I think the biggest priority really is to harness all the resources that are available in this country to reduce crime to prevent crime. At the moment we are not doing enough in harnessing the Social Services, Planners, Education, Youth and Community Service and all these voluntary organisations.' (Chief Superintendent)

A number of agency respondents spoke of the advantages of organisations working together, quoting their own experiences with the Police Consultative Group and inter-agency training. Both they and the community volunteers perceived the following benefits arising from closer collaboration:

(a) Improvements in their own effectiveness:

'I don't think in all honesty you can run any form of organisation efficiently without striving for co-operation with other agencies and organisations.' (Agency worker)

'There must be co-operation at all levels in city authorities, including the police. This co-operation must concern buildings, council housing, types of housing, where to put industrial estates, road planning and so on. All of this could be far better done with initial co-operation having had a study and then putting it down. After all, that example that you showed was typical. The increase in the number of offenders was going up because it was a new development. They had put too many young families in there.' (Community volunteer)

(b) Improved informal communication, thus avoiding tragedies such as the 'Maria Colwell' case. Both groups mentioned this particular case and blamed the failure on agencies restricting information flow, although there was also some disagreement as to how much information should be released to volunteers.

(c) Police expertise becoming available to other agencies:

'We have all identified, haven't we, that the police do a very good job of work . . . my suggestion is that it would be a very good idea if the police passed on some of their expertise to the social workers and the masses that they have in their field.' (Community volunteer)

(d) Obviating duplication of services and waste of resources.

(e) Reduction of planning mistakes.

Two disadvantages were also identified:

(i) Both agency workers and community volunteers feared that too much co-operation and co-ordination could lead to some agencies encroaching on the preserves of others (territorial violations):

' I don't see the police as being a substitute for Youth Leaders, Social Services and everything else that we seem to have in abundance, but are always missing when you need them . . .' (Community volunteer)

(ii) Police and community volunteers expressed fears that a policy of co-operation might lead to inaction, each agency sitting back waiting for someone else to assume leadership.

The senior officers were also very concerned about who should be responsible for *initiating* collaboration. They favoured the idea of the co-ordinator being appointed by the Government and thought the Home Office could 'pull the threads together'. After prolonged discussion they resisted proposals that the police should take the initiative:

'It's an invidious position for the police to be in to try and organise these agencies, as Colin Moore has been doing. This isn't a job for the police, the police should be one of these agencies that is being co-ordinated. Who can co-ordinate them in a matter of discussion.' (Chief Superintendent)

All agreed there were barriers to collaboration. The police groups were critical of social workers, accusing them of indecision and of lacking practical knowledge of children and family life. They also criticised the rapid turnover of social work staff; and the evangelical and offender-centred approaches of social workers and probation officers which too often ignored the need of victims:

'The social workers thought this kid would be violent so I went into the caravan and said to this kid, "Get out". He said, "Fuck off", so I just sort of helped him out of the caravan. I yanked him out of bed by his hair. No more trouble. But the social worker was convinced that he was a violent kid. He was only a mouthy little bugger but if that's the social worker for you what are they going to do with them?' (City centre constable)

'I mean your social worker. In the last two years I've had *eighteen different* social workers on my patch'. (Resident constable)

'A few weeks ago I had a case with a social worker who sat in on an interview I was having with three children. Mother had had umpteen husbands and she has now just married the nextdoor neighbour. He is an alcoholic. Afterwards the social worker said, "Father will be a good influence on those children. He's helping them with their homework" So I said, "Do you know anything about the father?" The social worker replied that she did not. So I told her, "He's an alcoholic, slept rough around the city for a number of years and has got a criminal record as long as your arm." The social worker expressed complete surprise. She didn't know this and she was going to report to a case meeting that everything was all right in the family.' (Resident constable)

'Take a mugger, a young boy hits an old lady over the head with a brick. All they're concerned with is the young boy. There is no sympathy for the old lady. They never see her.' (City centre constable)

'Social workers and probation officers aren't accepted by the majority in this country. They are seen as interfering old busybodies.' (Superintendent)

The anecdotes were numerous, highlighting the gaps in mutual understanding. When the question was put to the city centre constables that social workers and policemen could work together from the same building there was immediate hostility and violent rejection. Then one constable quoted from his own experience of a social worker sharing police experiences:

> 'I had these social worker students on attachment for a week in the back of my incident car. I noticed their attitude change so much through the week. They realised there is another side to the coin. I remember one job, I went to where an old lady had someone break into her house. The old lady had been threatened with a knife. The social worker was there seeing for herself the sort of terror that old people can suffer from. That was one social worker I worked with whose attitude changed by the end of the week . . . but once you've worked with them for a week, had meals with them, well, we start trusting each other, don't we?' (City centre constable)

This anecdote sparked off awareness of the benefits that could flow from shared work experiences, and completely changed the group's attitude, highlighting the importance that one officer with personal experience can have in modifying or even changing opinion. In this case, the group began to see the clear value of inter-agency placements in training and ended by recommending further development of placement schemes and inter-agency training to obviate conflict between agencies. Some also suggested a greater involvement with voluntary bodies, particularly at neighbourhood level to bring agencies together at a common focal point.

Conclusions

In sum, the need was generally accepted for police, statutory agencies and other organisations to work together, because it would lead to improved communications, better use of resources and the avoidance of planning mistakes. Whether this could be achieved was questionable, as many saw insurmountable barriers separating the so-called 'professional' agencies. It was those who had been involved in placements or inter-agency training who were able to convince the others that it was attainable. The vigorous arguments amongst senior officers as to who should co-ordinate the agencies revealed why the initiative had not been seized and exploited by the police in the past.

3. Relationships between Police and the Community
Finally, the groups discussed questions of relationships between police and community. All the policemen agreed that if a similar gulf developed between police and public in the way that now existed between agencies (and some believed it already had in some parts of the United Kingdom) then the police would become increasingly ineffective. One group thought it would mean the demise of policing by consent and the birth of policing by fear. It was a city centre policeman who offered the alternative:

> 'We have to concentrate on the prevention of crime; the more we prevent it the less there is for us to detect. I firmly believe that the best preventive measure that we can adopt is to put uniformed men out on the streets on foot; where they can get involved with people. Where the people accept the police presence as the norm. They are happy to talk to policemen. They are happy to pass information and the people generally welcome uniformed policemen amongst them.'

The community volunteers were equally emphatic on the types of relationship they wanted their policemen to develop. They variously described it as: helpful; approachable; involved; fatherly; headmasterly; friendly; fair; educated; human; counselling.

In order to develop this relationship they thought it would be necessary for policemen to exercise a sense of discretion when dealing with minor crimes and petty infringements of the law. The community volunteers and agency workers suggested that there were three areas in which policemen could use discretion. The first was by not resorting to official action over every incident. The second was for the local policeman personally to caution young people for minor crimes. There were repeated pleas that policemen should inform parents of erring children because too many parents were seen to be opting out of their responsibilities:

> 'I think there is a lot of value in having a resident policeman who might just caution young childen who had been shoplifting and they

know him. They know how far they can go, and then he says, "Right, I'll forget about it, if you do it again you'll be in court".' (Agency worker)

The third was by acting before events deteriorated into incidents of a more serious nature:

'When you see the possibility of something happening you should do something positive. Not wait for it to happen. When you see a group of kids hanging around a motor bike which doesn't belong to them, I would expect the policeman to take action; not just to walk away and wait until somebody jumps on it and attempts to ride it off.' (Community volunteer)

The same two groups expected the policeman to be able to switch from an authoritarian stance with the threat of coercive powers to that of a friendly figure who persuaded by example. They considered his stature in the community would depend on how well he acted out these dual roles, although some agency workers argued that it was impossible for a policeman to enact roles which were inherently in conflict. This argument was not accepted by the majority, who emphasised that most people play a variety of roles in the course of the day. The community volunteers described how their local constable demonstrates this ability. Significantly these were the only policemen they mentioned, thus giving the impression that the Exeter Police Division consisted of just fifteen men (the total number of resident constables). The following remarks were typical:

'We have a local policeman. David is tremendous. He's a good friend and he goes out of his way to help the community. He does more than his duty. The ordinary citizen doesn't really do his but David does more than his duty.'

'Our experience with our local policeman is just that. He's a friend. He's not only a policeman on the spot but he is a member of the community. He is also a member of the community association as an individual as well as the policeman on duty.'

'That one with the beard, he is great. Kids go up to him and speak. He walks in and out all the time at school. All the children respect him. He does sport with them and everything. They are not afraid of him. He is a policeman still.'

The resident constables themselves spoke of their job satisfaction playing dual roles. They described the variety of duties that they undertook:

Building up links with the community association.
Developing personal relationships with individuals.
Creating or supporting activities for young people.
Assisting other agency workers to accomplish their objectives.
Identifying, cautioning and counselling potential juvenile delinquents and their parents.
Enforcing the law.
Introducing other policemen (e.g. detectives) into the community.

There was general agreement that there are natural limitations to the service that the police can give the community. First, the fact that police will always be recognised as law enforcers. This in itself inhibits depth of relationships. Secondly, the problems that arise because the police service, communities and individuals all demanded different objectives for the police to accomplish. These objectives were often in conflict with each other, e.g. police efforts to solve a spate of street robberies could cause hostility if innocent people were subjected to harassment. Thirdly, the fact that police can rarely be there the very moment they are needed.

The resident constables went on to mention two other limitations placed upon them by the policies of other agencies, on the type of service that they wanted to give.

(i) Lack of understanding by local authorities of the need to develop or support local informal control systems:

> 'We've got nowhere to meet. No Community Centre. The council have just spent £38,000 to convert an old school to a Tramps' Hostel and they don't even come from Exeter. But when you want somewhere for the old ladies to meet, there is nothing for them. How can you weld a community together when you have to meet in each other's houses?' (Resident constable)

(ii) Unhelpful standards imposed by other agencies upon their volunteers, which either professionalised them or frightened them away! This made it difficult to 'activate the good':

'Then out comes the Youth and Community Service to say, we can't
do it because they have got to supply 'X' number of leaders. So I said
what about the voluntary workers? He said that they were not allowed
because they were not qualified. Now this is a load of rubbish – all they
have is a bit of paper to say they are qualified youth leaders, which
means nothing. They've got one little girl – just 21 years of age. She is
supposed to be a youth leader. 'She hasn't got a clue. Yet once some
senior kids say, "I'll come on the Wednesday night and run the
5-a-side football", they wouldn't let them. . . . If the local authority are
informed that you have got 70 kids coming along to your youth club
then they say you've got to have seven trained leaders, one to every ten
children.' (Resident constable)

Although approving an extended role for constables, the senior
officers worried about their own personal roles in developing
closer links with the community. This stemmed from personal
experiences gained from observing police/community relations in
another police force – where some had seen a Sub-Divisional
Commander developing personal relationships with community
leaders and minority groups. One Chief Superintendent described
it as seeing a man 'walking a tight rope'.

Conclusions
Whatever the difficulties, there was general agreement that police
must develop closer relationships with communities: and that it
was the *quality* of this relationship that gave the individual
policeman

(a) his *stature* in the community;
(b) his *ability to control* the community informally.

The inability to play these dual roles of friend and enforcer
would reduce police effectiveness and damage police-community
relations.

The development of formal and informal relationships also
meant police supporting or helping to create community institutions. The senior officers realised that they would need the active
assistance of other statutory agencies, both at local and central
government level, and that this meant developing links with those
they had often criticised.

It was generally concluded that the strength and effectiveness of all statutory agencies comes from the way they listen to and support the community. If they are inefficient or destructively bureaucratic they destroy the very controls which policemen see as vital to the wellbeing of society. Inevitably then, the strength and effectiveness of the police service must relate to its ability to use community resources. To put it another way, policing is a task not for police alone but for society as a whole.

8. Reflections and Conclusions

Analysis of the CPSU projects and the many comments made about them pose fundamental questions about future policing practices in this country. It is said that the police are at the crossroads and that as a matter of urgency, they must choose what form of policing will take them into the twenty-first century. Unfortunately, there are no crossroads and no single decision will decide which path will be taken. Policing will no doubt continue to develop gradually, influenced by a host of decisions. Some of these decisions will be made by policemen of all ranks from constable to Chief HMI; others will come from outside the service – from commentators, communities and politicians. What is vital to the debate is that everyone who has the power to influence developments should be aware of the issues involved, and the alternative paths that can be followed.

Primary to the quality of life in a community is its sense of personal security. This may be influenced more by crime than by anything else. And here, there are two major factors. First, that people react to their *perceptions* of crime rather than to the facts. For example, if they feel that crime in their community is a serious problem, then there will be a great deal of alarm and public comment, with pressures on the police and judiciary to do something about it, even if crime rates are *not* increasing.

Secondly, built into each of our communities is a critical breaking point at which the public will no longer accept crime. Up to this point they will tolerate some crime, but that does not mean that they necessarily approve of it.

These two factors help to explain phenomena which have been witnessed in several villages in Devon and Cornwall. The inhabitants have 'perceived' an increase in crime and this has resulted in newspaper headlines that the streets in the villages are unsafe or, for example, caused an irate farmer to threaten reprisals against a problem family whom he identified as perpetrators of crime. Such was the public concern in each case that the police were forced to consider the 'problem'. Analysis of known crime usually showed that it was either decreasing or about the same. But in the eyes of the villagers the increase was *real*, and as a result, they felt they had reached breaking point. This is why people in small Devon villages can become more upset about their crime rate than the inhabitants of an inner city area who are certainly subject to much more crime.

In such circumstances, what can and should the police do? Can they afford to ignore the situation because there is no numerical increase in crime? Many would argue that as there is no threat there is no danger. Furthermore, there are those who claim that crime is positively functional for a society because it provides an occasion for people to unite against a common enemy, e.g. the French sociologist Emile Durkheim argues in *The Divisions of Labour in Society* (1) that people react to crime by increasing their social contacts and pulling together, thereby enhancing the solidarity of the community. Similar views are expounded by George Simmel (2) and Lewis Coser (3). If this is so, why then did such communities as Pruitt Igoe and the Piggeries disintegrate? As the inhabitants of those communities perceived crime increasing around them, so they became more and more fearful and suspicious of each other. People stayed in their homes. Neighbours became strangers. People resorted to their own devices to defend themselves and abdicated their responsibilities to prevent crime, leaving it to the police. This action reduced public support for the police, and as the communities became more aware of this trend, so people were more likely to commit crime because of the lower risk of arrest.

It therefore appears that crime reduces *trust* and the *sense of security*. A growing feeling of estrangement from the environment reduces solidarity, weakening informal social control systems. This in turn weakens the restraints on criminal behaviour, leading to higher crime rates, and gradually the community becomes disorganised and fragments. No community is safe from this threat because the crucial factors are inhabitants' perceptions rather than actual levels of crime.

Conklin (4) in his book *The Impact of Crime* gives several examples of how crime creates disorganised communities. One example is taken from Truman Capote's account of four people murdered in a small American town. Conklin writes that

Durkheim would have suggested that the inhabitants 'would wax indignant in common, unite as a group and come together to talk about the crime'. Yet Capote's account clearly shows that initially people disbelieved the crime, then turned their suspicions against their neighbours. There was an upsurge in people adopting defensive measures, such as purchasing firearms and new locks, or keeping house lights on to scare criminals away. Even when the murderers – two ex-convicts – were caught, anxiety did not immediately diminish, but only gradually subsided, leaving a residue of distrust and guilt. Conklin goes on to suggest that a recurrence of such crimes in the same community would gradually recreate distrust and suspicion, culminating in a fragmented community.

Conklin gives similar examples which detail how communities have reacted to the problems of adolescent drug use and homosexuality; and together these clearly show that even relatively homogeneous communities can be divided by crime, and that this tendency is exacerbated in communities comprising a mixture of racial and ethnic groups. In brief, his evidence suggests that Durkheim's postulation that crime brings people together is not generally valid.

If this is so, and my experience certainly support this proposition, then it follows that the police service should recognise:

1. That the most important crime control forces in society are those in its informal control systems.
2. That people react mainly to their perceptions of crime.
3. That there is a crime tolerance level above which the community will not accept increases.
4. That once the tolerance is reached, then the threat of crime can, if allowed to go unchecked, fragment a community by creating an atmosphere of suspicion, distrust, hostility and estrangement from both the environment and the police.
5. That some of the traditional reactive policing responses may only inflame a deteriorating atmosphere, e.g. by warning people to fortify their homes with watchdogs, bars or alarms, police may help to create barriers between people, and to reduce social interaction.

Failure to recognise these factors has meant that the police service has neglected to use or help strengthen these controlling forces and has done little to exploit this area of social crime prevention. And if the police over-react with traditional responses then they may undermine their chance to mobilise or to activate those innate controlling forces in communities. Over-reaction may even help destroy the very forces that need to be built on and supported. Moreover, if the police insist on operating without community consent, then their efforts may well be at best wasted, or at worst, inflammatory.

Policing should therefore remain a negotiated contract between the public and the police so that they both identify that the main-tenance of law is a co-operative rather than a delegated responsi-bility. The police, on their side, must do what they can to put back into the hands of the citizens problems of control in their communities, whilst society on its side must recognise that the making of communities capable of containing crime is a task for all, and that crime control is not the sole province of the police.

At the same time, it is no more than realistic to recognise that community activation is not immediately possible in the areas where there has been a history of social disorder. Such is the complexity of social problems in certain areas that individual agencies only appear to perpetuate traditions of hopelessness. These areas are the breeding grounds for many of the problems facing the police in their everyday work. Action in them is fraught with difficulty, and often results in criticism for either over- or under-reaction. Yet it is precisely these areas that are in most need of integrated agency/community action.

Though it is becoming increasingly clear to the great majority of those working in different agencies that co-operation and joint action is needed to deal with problems of delinquency, why is it then, when so many recognise this need, that it is not occurring? The fact is that, for a variety of reasons, not least the development of their own 'professionalism', policemen, social workers and other local authority representatives have grown remote not only from their communities but also from each other. This lessens each agency's chance to be effective, and permits conflicting policies to emerge which often work to mutual disadvantage.

Our experience suggests that to overcome these barriers, agencies should examine their policies to ensure they are not in conflict with those of other agencies or with community interests. They should also recognise what improvements are being made in the interests of each organisation rather than in those of the citizens for whom they are ostensibly introduced; that the failure to supply resources at community level is a threat to informal control systems; and that the urge to 'sanitise' community volunteers by rules and regulations often inhibits self-help. Social workers and others all too clearly erode people's innate abilities to cope, and this then contributes to the common malaise of inadequacy and apathy exhibited by many of our communities. Moreover, regulations such as those which insist that a mother who aspires to be an assistant in a playgroup must first go on a course before being allowed near the children can mean the loss of a volunteer, or even worse, that she withdraws because of lack of confidence. This is damaging both to the individual and the community.

Lack of motivation or will to come together often seems to stem from the existence of social and professional barriers between the different agencies. Professionalism here provides a two-edged weapon; whilst it can claim to develop skills and standards and relevant bodies of knowledge it must also plead guilty to erecting barriers to both understanding and co-operation. The barriers are real and daunting, comprising a mixture of hostility, suspicion, narrow mindedness and downright incompetence. Unfortunately, these are sometimes products of blinkered workers who often hide their own personal deficiencies behind the official designation of their profession so that the whole organisation becomes tainted by them.

A starting point for policemen and for other workers is that no one agency holds the answer to preventing crime, but that each agency is capable of some policing. By working together, not only do the agencies become more effective, but they come to appreciate each other's roles.

The suggestion that agencies work together is only the first step. The second step is apparent if one accepts the proposition that the statutory agencies, including the police, cannot even together contain crime and/or delinquency by themselves. Crime and delinquency can only be prevented *in* the community: and this means that agencies have to develop expertise in helping communities' own resources. This will be to reverse recent trends in which agencies take functions away from ordinary people – strategies which cripple communities because they breed human apathy and encourage citizens to opt out of their responsibilities. Any belief and expectation that the payment of 'Danegeld' in the way of taxes is all that is needed to absolve people of community responsibility is pure illusion. Danegeld cannot even provide a bare minimum of resources.

The Exeter experience demonstrates that people wish to become involved in their local problems, and that they have the ability to alleviate those of crime and delinquency. Their statements emphasise that they have far more faith in their own abilities than those of the politicians or those of the statutory agencies. There is clearly a wealth of untapped self-help within the neighbourhoods which, if found and harnessed in the right ways, will strengthen communities' capability to regulate themselves. But first, people must be helped to feel that they can control their environment to some degree. In doing so, they begin to feel more secure and this improves the quality of their lives.

The notion of helping to develop community resources is a tough pill for many professionals to swallow, however, and like many other professions the police service has great difficulty in accepting or using volunteers. This is typified in the way the police have allowed the Special Constabulary (unpaid volunteers who assist the regular force in times of emergencies or as directed) to decline in strength. The numbers of volunteers in the early 1920s were in excess of 200,000 whilst now they number less than 20,000. Undoubtedly, one of the causes for the decline is the continuing battle of 'professional versus volunteer' (which unhappily aflicts most professions), which is often fought with sarcasm, malice and slur in the letter columns of police magazines.

The thought that laymen may be more effective frightens most professionals. But all those in 'care and order' agencies must recognise the need to encourage communities to develop their will and capacities for *self* care and *self* order. The CPSU projects demonstrate this can be done in a number of ways or, for example, by 'public spirited' people volunteering to help the police as Specials in *their* neighbourhoods.

Whilst there is a clear need for a general strategy on these lines, it is equally clear that tactics will vary from area to area. Each separate area demands a separate contract between police and public. This means developing an approach based on empathy with the particular *needs and demands of that community.*

But there are also dangers to be emphasised. The *first* is that many police forces will consider the formation of a specialist community relations department to be sufficient for the new role. The point here is that the police service cannot afford to allow such a primary task to become the preserve of a very few; a specialism which would inevitably lead to it becoming a sub-culture within a sub-culture, debased and isolated from main-stream policing. *Second* are the dangers of the use of empirical research. Analysing local social and economic problems brings new influence to those that have the power to affect or even control people's lives – the City Planner, Housing Manager and others; and it also helps individuals to understand or cope with their environments. But at the same time this form of demography is an explosive mixture which must be handled with great care and understanding. In the hands of insensitive people it can be used as an instrument to repress or to stigmatise. If used solely for reactive policing then it will simply produce a self-fulfilling prophecy of crime and deviance. *Third* are the dangers that policemen will not develop a balanced approach to policing, i.e. they will concentrate on either preventive or reactive policies which, if carried to their ultimate conclusions, could be counter-productive in creating unbalanced strategies. *Fourth* are the dangers that the sheer professionalism of the police service will continue to disable the community by:

(a) Failing to encourage volunteers.
(b) Making people believe that problems of crime and delinquency are too great for ordinary people to cope with.

Fifth, and arguably the most dangerous, is that in carrying out the pro-active role the police come to believe they are filling what they see as a leadership void in present-day society. This assumption could blow back in their faces and create distress and conflict rather than harmony between agencies and within communities. The policeman's leadership qualities, recognised by many in the community, must be subdued so that they are seen in terms of 'service' rather than as a new velvet glove on the old iron hand; a more insidious form of social control. There are real dangers here; and this research makes it apparent that whilst communities, agencies and politicians are prepared to accept police as initiators, moderators and catalysts, they may well be fearful of police claiming 'leadership' roles which challenge their own status or capabilities.

However, if the police service accepts the challenge of developing closer links with other agencies and using community resources, then it will certainly help to dispel their image as supporters of the 'status quo' and help them return to their original traditions of identity with the community.

Sir Robert Mark (5) speaking at the Police Staff College recently commented: 'We who are the anvil on which society beats out the problems and abrasions of social inequality, race prejudice, weak laws and ineffective legislation should not be inhibited from expressing our views whether critical or constructive.' Thus the police cannot ignore the challenge presented by many examples of failure in social policies and urban planning. Their traditional political neutrality means that the British policeman can descend into the political arena to enact the role Mark advocates. But it is important that if they do, police statements on crime and associated problems are based on empirical evidence and not on emotional convictions. Preventive policing starts with changing a neighbourhood's perception of its crime, and with creating higher tolerance levels. These can only be accomplished by the use of hard data.

The approach now being developed by the Devon and Cornwall police forms a model here. It can be summarised as follows:

(a) To compile and present empirical crime data on specific geographical localities.

(b) To consider alternative ways for the police to deal with problems and to make a choice between them.
(c) To approach other agencies in their communities with knowledge relevant to their problems.
(d) To present them with relevant data.
(e) To stimulate discussions of the issues and of alternative solutions.
(f) To support community decisions.

The CPSU experiences suggest the following practical policy recommendations:-

That police should:
(i) Recognise the full implications of preventive and reactive approaches to policing.
(ii) Aim to achieve an appropriate balance between the two approaches. This will necessitate a revaluation of policing priorities, taking into account community circumstances, needs and views.
(iii) Develop an analytical system that produces data capable of being used both by police and by other statutory agencies.
(iv) Improve the status of the resident home beat or community constable so that he is recognised by the police service as its primary functionary.
(v) Reassess present police training methods to help extend policy and practice beyond the narrow fields of reactive policing.
(vi) Aim to support community institutions and organisations.
(vii) Act as a catalyst to develop co-ordination between statutory agencies in ways that ensure that social policies and practice help to prevent crime.

To make these points is not to deny the importance of enforcement. Enforcement in itself is an essential means of preventing crime – one of many which police employ. However, if police develop their enforcement policies at the expense of preventive policies, dangers increase of them losing the sympathy, support and active co-operation of the public.

The greatest challenge facing the police service in Britain today is thus whether it can develop strategies which harmonise preventive and reactive approaches, and create balances between them appropriate to the varying needs of local communities in different parts of the country. At an individual level, the test of a policeman's effectiveness is likely to be the ways in which he can both enforce the law and develop preventive activity with other agencies and with the people of the community he serves. In brief, both for the individual policeman and for the police organisation as a whole, the acid test of effectiveness will be their capability to use all available means and resources at their disposal to achieve their primary task: to keep the peace.

References

Chapter 1

1. Wilkins, L. 'The Prevention of Crime', NACRO Paper No. 10, 1974, pp. 14–21.

2. Wheeler, S. Task Force report on Juvenile Delinquency and Youth Crime to the President's Commission in Law Enforcement and Administration of Justice. US Government Printing Office, 1967.

3. Home Office Working Paper. Extrapolated from *A Review of Criminal Justice Policy, 1976*, HMSO, 1977.

4. Newman, O. *Defensible Space*, Architectural Press, 1972, p. 1.

5. Jacobs, J. *Death and Life of Great American Cities*, Penguin Books, 1961, p. 41.

6. Banton, M. 'Policing a Divided Society', *The Police Journal*, 47, pp. 304–321.

7. Brown, J. 'The Primary Object of an Efficient Police', *The Cranfield Papers*, Peel Press, 1978.

8. Alderson, J. 'Resources to Ideas', Devon and Cornwall Constabulary, 1977.

9. Alderson, J. 'The Fulcrum', *Police Federation Magazine*, Vol. 8, No. 8, April 1976, pp. 16/23.

Chapter 2

1. Newman, O. *Defensible Space, Op. cit*, pp. 111–112.

2. Jacobs, J. *Death and Life of Great American Cities, Op. cit.*, p. 258.

3. Jones, H. 'Approaches to an Ecological Study', *British Journal of Delinquency*, Vol. 8, 1958, pp. 277–293.

4. McClintock. 'The Dark Figure', *Collected Studies in Criminological Research*. Council of Europe, Vol. 5, 1970, pp. 7–34.

Chapter 3

1. Newman, O. 'Vandalism', BBC Film.

2. Yancey, W.L. 'Architecture, Inter-action and Social Control' in *Urban Man*, ed. J. Helmer and N. Eddington, The Free Press, New York, 1973, p. 111.

3. Moore, W. *The Vertical Ghetto*, Random House, 1969.

4. Taylor, L. *Signs of Trouble*, BBC Publication, 1976, p. 40.

5. Linton, R. *The Study of Man*, Appleton-Century-Crofts, 1964.

6. Homans, G.C. *The Human Group*, Routledge & Kegan Paul, 1975.

7. *Op. cit.*
   7. *Op. cit.*
8. Young, M. and Willmott, P. *Family and Kinship in East London*, Nicholls, 1957.

9. Zimbardo, P. 'The Human Choice', *Urban Man*, Helmer and Eddington, New York, 1973.

10. Foster, B. Report in possession of author, 1977.

Chapter 4

1. Blaber, Ann. 'The Exeter Community Policing Consultative Group: a study of the first year.' National Association for the Care and Resettlement of Offenders, 1979.

Chapter 5

1. Police Federation Pamphlet, 1976.

2. *Social Work Today*, Vol. 7, No. 8, 8 July 1976, p. 225.

3. *Ibid.*, p. 232.

4. *Ibid.*, p. 230.

5. Bush, S. 'Hello, Hello, Hello', *Community Care*, 10 August 1978, p. 37.

Chapter 8

1. Durkheim, E. *The Division of Labour in Society*, translated by George Simpson, Glencoe Three, The Free Press, 1933.

2. Simmel, G. Cited in Lewis Coser, *The Functions of Social Conflict*. Glencoe Three, The Free Press, 1956.

3. Coser, L. *Ibid.*

4. Conklin, J.E. *The Impact of Crime*, Macmillan, 1975, pp. 50–68.

5. Mark, Sir Robert. *Policing a Perplexed Society*, Allen & Unwin, 1977.

Bibliography

ACKROYD, C. et al. *The Technology of Political Control*, Penguin Books, 1976.

ANGEL, S. *Discouraging Crime Through City Planning*, University of California, Berkeley, 1968.

BAGLEY, C. 'Juvenile Delinquency in Exeter', *Urban Studies*, 2, pp. 33–50.

BALDWIN, J. 'British Areal Studies of Crime: An Assessment', *British Journal of Criminology*, 15, 1975.

BANTON, M. *The Policeman in the Community*, Tavistock, 1964.

BECKER, H. *Outsiders: Studies in the Sociologies of Deviance*, New York Free Press, 1963.

BELSON, W.A. *The Public and the Police*, Harper & Row, 1975.

BOWES, S. *The Police and Civil Liberties*, Laurence & Wishart, 1966.

BRIAR, S. & PILIAVIN, I.M. 'Delinquency, Situational Inducements and Commitment to Conformity', *Social Problems*, 13, pp. 35–40, 1965.

BROWN, J. 'Shades of Grey', Cranfield Institute, 1977.

BROWN, J. & HOWES, G. (ed.) *The Police and the Community*, Saxon House, 1975.

BROWN, M.J. et al. 'Criminal Offences in an Urban Area and their Associated Social Variables', *British Journal of Criminology*, 12, pp. 250–68, 1972.

BURT, C. *The Young Delinquents*, University of London Press, 1944.

BUTT, R. 'Is the Social Revolution Over?' *Sunday Times*, 15 August 1976.

CAIN, M. *Society and the Policeman's Role*, Routledge & Kegan Paul, 1974.

CHAPPLE, N.L. 'Kirkby New Town – An Objective Assessment of Social Economic and Police Problems'. Limited publication, Merseyside Police, 1975.

CHATTERTON, M. *The Police in Social Control*, Institute of Criminology, Cambridge University Press, 1976.

CHILTON, R.J. 'Continuity in Delinquency Research: A Comparison of Studies for Baltimore, Detroit and Indianapolis', *American Sociological Review* 29, pp. 71–83, 1972.

CLARKE, R.V.G. & MARTIN, D.N. *Absconding from Approved Schools*, HMSO, 1971.

CLIFFORD, W. 'Crime as a Problem for Research in a Developmental Perspective', *Justice of the Peace*, 138, pp. 703–4, 1974.

CLOWARD, R.A. & OHLIN, L.E. *Delinquency and Opportunity*, Routledge & Kegan Paul, 1961.

COHEN, S. 'Directions for Research on Adolescent Group Violence and Vandalism', *British Journal of Criminology* 11, pp. 319–40, 1971.

CORNISH, D.B. & CLARKE, R.V.G. *Residential Treatment and Its Effects on Delinquency*, HMSO, 1975.

COX, B. *Civil Liberties in Britain*, Penguin Books, 1975.

COX, W.H. *Cities – the Public Dimension*, Penguin Books, 1976.

CUMBERBATCH, G. 'Fear of Crime'. Lecture at Annual Meeting of the British Association for Advancement of Science, 1977.

CUMMING, E., CUMMING, I. & EDELL, L. 'The Policeman as Philosopher, Guide and Friend', *Social Problems* 12, p. 276, 1964.

DAVIS, F.J. 'Crime News in Colorado Newspaper', *American Journal of Sociology*, LVII, pp. 325–30, January 1952.

DE ALARCON, R. 'Lessons from the Recent British Drug Outbreak'. Anglo-American Conference on Drug Dependence, Royal Society of Medicine, April 1973.

DOWNES, D.M. *The Delinquent Solution*, Routledge & Kegan Paul, 1966.

DURANT, R. *Watling – A Survey of Social Life on a New Housing Estate*, King & Son, 1939.

EASTHOPE, G. *History of Social Research Methods*, Longman, 1974.

EDWARDS, A. 'Sex and Area Variations in Delinquency Rates in an English City', *British Journal of Criminology*, 13, pp. 121–37, 1973.

EVANS, P. 'The Black Man's Burden', *The Times*, 30 January 1978.

FOOTE, W. *Street Corner Society*, University of Chicago Press, 1943.

FRANKENBURGH, R. *Communities in Britain*, Penguin Books, 1966.

GIBBONS, D.C. 'Observations on the Study of Crime Causation', *American Journal of Sociology*, 77, pp. 262–78, 1971.

GOFFMAN, E. *Relations in Public*, Allen Lane, 1971.

GOLDSTEIN, H. *Policing a Free Society*, Ballinger, 1977.

GOULD, L.C. 'The Changing Structure of Property Crime in an Affluent Society', *Social Forces*, 48, pp. 50–59, 1969.

GRENOUGH, J.L. 'Crime Prevention; A New Approach', *Journal of Police Science and Administration*, 2, pp. 339–43, 1974.

HALL, S. et al. *Policing the Crisis*, Macmillan, 1978.

HILLMAN, M. & WHALLEY, A. *Fair Play for All*, PEP Broadsheet No. 571, 1977.

HOLMAN, R. (ed.) *Socially Deprived Families in Britain*, Bedford Square Press, 1970.

HOOD, R. (ed.) *Crime, Criminology and Public Policy*. Essays in honour of Sir Leon Radzinowicz, Heinemann, 1974.

HONEYCOMBE, G. *Adam's Tale*, Hutchinson, 1974.

HUMPHREY, D. *Police Power and Black People*, Panther, 1972.

ILLICH, I. et al. *Disabling Professions*, Boyars, 1977.

JAMES, L. 'The Police Service and the Future', *Justice of the Peace*, 13 September 1975.

JEFFERY, C.R. *Crime Prevention through Environmental Design*, Beverley Hills, Sage Publications, 1971.

JONES, H. *Crime in a Changing Society*, Penguin Books, 1965.

KINGSBURY, A. 'A Comparative Study of Educational Programs for Crime Prevention in England and the United States'. University Microfilms International, Ann Arbor, Michigan, UM76–2616–Z6146.

KRAUZE, E. & MILLER, S.H. *Social Research Design*, Longman, 1974.

LAMBERT, J. *Crime, Police and Race Relations*, Institute of Race Relations, Oxford University Press, 1970.

LANDERS, B. *Towards an Understanding of Juvenile Delinquency*, New York, Columbia University Press, 1954.

LONGFORD, Lord. *Pornography – the Longford Report*, Coronet, 1972.

MACK, J.A. *The Crime Industry*, Saxon House, 1975.

MARSH, A. 'Race, Community and Anxiety', *New Society*, 23 February 1973.

MARTIN, J.P. & WILSON, G. *The Police: A Study in Manpower*, Heinemann, 1969.

MATZA, D. *Delinquency and Drift*, New York, Wiley, 1964.

MAYHEW, P. et al. *Crime as Opportunity*, Home Office Research Study No. 34, 1976.

MAYS, J.B. *Crime and Its Treatment*, Longman, 1970.

MAYS, J.B. (ed.) *Juvenile Delinquency, the Family and the Social Group*, Longman, 1972.

McCABE, S. & SUTCLIFFE, F. *Defining Crime*, Blackwell, 1978.

METHODIST RECORDER, 'Police and Community Crisis', 3 November 1977.

MERTON, K. *Social Theory and Social Structure*, Glencoe, Illinois, The Free Press, 1957.

MINTO, G.A. *The Thin Blue Line*, Hodder & Stoughton, 1965.

MORRIS, N. & HAWKINS, G. *The Honest Politician's Guide to Crime Control*, University of Chicago Press, 1970.

MORRIS, T. *The Criminal Area*, Routledge & Kegan Paul, 1959.

MOSSE, G.L. (ed.) *Police Forces in History*, Beverley Hills, Sage Publications, 1975.

NEIBURG, H.L. 'Crime Prevention by Urban Design', *New Society*, 12, pp. 41–47, 1974.

POWER, M.J. et al. 'Neighbourhood, School and Juveniles Before the Court', *British Journal of Criminology*, 12, pp. 111–32, 1972.

PRESS, S.J. *Some Effects of an Increase in Police Manpower in the Twentieth Precinct of New York City*, New York, Rand, 1971.

PUGH, HICKSON & HINDINGS (ed.) *Writers on Organisation*, Penguin Books, 1971.

PYLE, F.G. et al. *The Spatial Dynamics of Crime*, Chicago University Press, 1974.

QUINNEY, R. *The Social Reality of Crime*, Boston, Little Brown, 1970.

RADZINOWICZ, L. *Ideology and Crime*, New York, Columbia University Press, 1966.

RADZINOWICZ & KING. *The Growth of Crime*, Hamish Hamilton, 1977.

REISS, A.J. *The Police and the Public*, New Haven, Yale University Press, 1971.

REISS, A.J. 'Stuff and Nonsense about Social Surveys and Observations', in H. S. Becker et al, *Institution and the Person*, pp. 351–67, Aldine Press, 1968.

ROWLAND, J. *Community Decay*, Penguin Books, 1973.

SCHMID, C.F. 'Urban Crime Areas, Part I', *American Sociology Review*, 25, pp. 527–42, 1960.

SCHMID, C.F. 'Urban Crime Areas, Part II', *American Sociology Review*, 25, pp. 655–78.

SELLITZ, et al. *Research Methods in Social Relations*, Methuen, 1965.

SHAW, C.R. & McKAY, M.D. *Juvenile Delinquency and Urban Areas*, Chicago University Press, revised ed., 1969.

SHEFFIELD. *Police Inquiry*. HMSO, Cmnd. 2176, November 1963.

SKOLNICK, J.H. 'Justice Without Trial', *Law Enforcement in a Democratic Society*, Wiley, 1966.

SPARKS, R.F., GENN, H.G. & DODD, D.J. *Surveying Victims*, Wiley, 1977.

WADE, A.L. 'Social Processes in the Act of Vandalism', in Clinard, M.B. & Quinney, E.T. (ed.), *Criminal Behaviour Systems: A Typology*, New York, Holt, Rinehart & Winston, 1967.

WEST, D.J. *Who Becomes Delinquent?* Heinemann, 1975.

WILKS, J.A. 'Ecological Correlates of Crime and Delinquency'. Appendix A in the President's Commission on Law Enforcement and Administration of Justice, *Task Force Report on Crime and its Impact – an Assessment*, Washington, DC, US. Government Printing Office, 1967.

WILKINS, L.T. *Social Deviance*, Tavistock, 1964.

WILSHER, P. & RIGHTER, R. *The Exploding Cities*, Deutsch, 1975.

WILSON, R. *Difficult Housing Estates*, Tavistock, 1963.

WOLFENDEN REPORT. *The Future of Voluntary Organisations*, Croom Helm, 1978.

WOOD, E. 'Housing Design – A Social Theory', New York Citizens Housing and Planning Council, 1961.

YOUNG, J. 'The Role of the Police as Amplifiers of Deviancy, Negotiators of Reality and Translators of Fantasy', in *Images of Deviance*, ed. S. Cohen, Penguin Books, 1971.

Appendix A
Research Methods used in Assessing CPSU's projects

Because of the inexperience of the CPSU personnel, no assessment procedures were built into the projects they initiated. I was therefore faced with the problems of compensating for this omission in my research and I attempted to do this by using a number of separate, but reinforcing, methods. The results obtained revealed a number of common issues and thus identified a number of keys to thought and practice in this sphere of preventive policing.

The following methods were used:

1. Participant Observation
As the author of this report I took some active part in every CPSU project from 1976 to 1979. Obviously the way that I perceived the happenings affects my description of the specific projects. The very fact that I was emotionally involved created bias, as these were personal experiences. And my initial assumptions (after seventeen years as an operational detective) were cynical. I firmly believed the public to be apathetic; that most workers in other statutory agencies were hostile to police; and that law and order depended on one controlling factor – the level of police resources. Time and time again in the course of the last three years those assumptions have been proved wrong; and it was this chastening experience that caused me to question the whole strategy of present-day policing in England. Questioning that required the support of empirical evidence.

2. Personal Interviews
My second method was to interview key personnel who had been involved in the CPSU projects. These projects involved people from such agencies as the police, social and probation services, planners and the community. Analysing what they said revealed

areas of agreement and disagreement on the role of police in society and identified the major issues involved.

3. Attitude Survey

Thirdly, a questionnaire was formulated to discover what a representative sample of people from various agencies thought about certain major issues:

(a) The police role, which included its preventive and reactive functions.
(b) The role of statutory agencies in relation to preventive policing.
(c) The use of data in relation to preventive policing.

During the administration of the questionnaire visual empirical data was also displayed to the respondents. This material was based on the CPSU's research in Exeter, which is described in Chapter 3. However, to obviate bias, the evidence was displayed as being compiled about a fictitious town named Cranfield. The reason for this display was to give all the respondents the same factual knowledge on which they could formulate their opinions. This approach helped to overcome the myth, gossip and part knowledge that some or all of the respondents may have held about the work of the CPSU.

It is accepted that opinions and attitudes are subject to constant variation and can change at a moment's notice. What were sought in the responses were those relating to the experiences and activities of the CPSU in which I had also been deeply involved.

Some of the statements on which the attitude scales were based were drawn from newspapers and periodicals; some from personal experiences at public meetings and police training centres.

There were also a number of open-ended questions which sought both opinion and factual responses. This was to allow the respondents freedom to decide the form, detail and length of answers. Furthermore, it enriched the quality of the response material.

4. Structured Discussion

Following the administration of the structured questionnaire, the groups of respondents replicated the view of their own peer group by discussing in forum three key topics:

(a) The priorities of the police.
(b) Relationships between police and other statutory agencies.
(c) Relationship between police and the community.

By using this technique, the interviewer was able to probe more deeply into what and how the respondents felt about these particular themes.

These discussions, which lasted from half an hour to an hour, were noted by the interviewer and tape recorded. To try to obviate bias by the author the police discussion groups were supervised by an independent person.

Sample Population

The respondents were drawn from three groups – police, statutory agencies and communities. For ease of handling and to ensure that a cross-section of opinion was obtained, these three groups in turn were divided into a number of sub-categories.

1. Police

Present-day police personnel can be divided into three main categories. First there are those involved in management, secondly those involved in reactive policing and lastly, those who carry out predominantly preventive duties. To ensure that a comparison could be made of the opinions held by these very different categories with their different tasks and responsibilities, three representative groups were formed.

(a) *Senior officers* were chosen by the 'lottery method' from all who held the ranks of Chief Superintendent and Superintendent in the Devon and Cornwall Constabulary. Administratively they were handled in two groups, but their results were combined. Police Chief Superintendents are in charge of large territorial divisions or departments (e.g. Traffic or Personnel). They have considerable control over the deployment of police resources and are also instrumental in implementing the Chief Constable's policies. Obviously the extent to which they implement these is subject to personal bias.

Superintendents usually assist Chief Superintendents in the management of a division or they control large sub-divisions, such as a city. In addition they also undertake investigative duties into serious crime or complaints against policemen.

Seven out of the eight chosen Chief Superintendents took part in the research discussions; their ages ranged from 50 to 59, with an average length of service of 29 years. Nine out of the ten randomly selected Superintendents responded to the invitation; their age range being 40 to 49 years, with an average length of service of $24\frac{1}{2}$ years.

(b) *Resident constables* are known in other forces as 'Home Beat Officers', 'Community Constables' or 'Neighbourhood Constables'. They carry out a variety of duties each day which can range from involvement in a youth club to executing arrest warrants. They have the opportunity to forge links with their community and to perform both preventive and reactive policing. Most of their duties are accomplished in the same locality on foot or by bicycle. These officers have a good deal of discretion in choosing their own hours of duty.

A sampling frame comprising the names of all such officers was compiled from the personnel of the Exeter Sub-Division. Ten policemen were chosen by the lottery method. Eight took part in the research discussions, two having to withdraw at the last moment because of duty commitments. Their age range was 30 to 39 years with an average length of service of $12\frac{1}{2}$ years.

(c) *City centre constables* have to work a shift system and are on call to answer emergencies throughout the city. They deal with a variety of jobs, such as accidents, drunks and shoplifters. Their work is usually reactive, with only conflict contact with the public; they have little chance to forge community contact.

A sampling frame was compiled of all the names of constables who perform these duties in Exeter Sub-Division. Ten respondents were selected to attend. Eight attended on the day, two being absent because of duty commitments. Their age range was 30 to 39 years with an average length of service of 7¾ years.

2. Statutory Agencies

These respondents were not representative of a particular agency, but chosen from a cross-section of local authority workers who were involved in some way in the care and order of a community. To ensure a cross-section of responses they were drawn from two different levels in their organisation – middle management and grass roots.

The first invitation was given to a number of representatives from different agencies who had been meeting at middle-management level over a period of twelve months as the result of a police initiative. Invitations were also issued to five specific agencies to send two workers from each with face-to-face contact with the community. Unlike the middle-management group, these workers had not come into contact with each other.

	Middle Management	Grass Roots
Probation	1	2
Housing	1	2
Education		2
Social Workers		2
Youth and Community	1	1
Politician	1	
Planner	1	
NACRO	1	
Police	2	
Total	8	9

They attended in their two groups on separate occasions and it was found that the age range of the middle managers was 40 to 49 years as compared with 30 to 39 years for the grass-roots workers. The managers' average length of service was fifteen years as compared with the others of six years.

3. Community Groups

Respondents in this group were drawn from people who had experience of community work at local level.

Five official community associations in Exeter were selected by the lottery method and invited to send two representatives. An approach was also made to those volunteer groups who had come together to create community activity in response to police pleas. Their unofficial leaders were asked to select two or three representatives to attend the discussion. All told, twenty-one representatives attended in two groups. The age range of the official community groups was 40 to 49 years as compared with 30 to 39 years amongst the 'new' volunteer representatives.

Pre-Test and Piloting of Research Instruments

Pre-testing of specific questions took place informally with colleagues and friends. After the questionnaire was compiled it was piloted on two occasions. This was to catch and solve unforeseen problems in its administration, such as the phasing and sequence of questions or its length. As the respondents would differ in education, temperament and opinion the selected test groups contained people of similar characteristics to those to be interviewed. They also came from an area which would not bring them into contact with the respondents who would be eventually sampled. As a result of the piloting only minor alterations had to be made by adding some open questions and also by clarifying existing questions.

Tabulation

Following the administering of the questionnaire a composite of primary data was compiled for each of the main groups. One master copy was compiled on all the police respondents, but composites were also made on the three sub-categories (senior officers, city centre and resident constables). This ensured that the police could be looked at in terms of individual groups or as a whole.

The final comparative tables were calculated with the use of 'means' and simple percentages. To ensure the elimination of errors both the primary data and tables were checked on three separate occasions by use of an electronic calculator. The tables can be found in Appendix C.

When analysing the peer groups' discussions, I sought to identify:

1. Continuity of content (the themes in the questionnaire which were later picked up in the discussion).
2. Those themes on which there was general agreement.
3. Those themes on which there was general disagreement.

Appendix B
Descriptive List of Empirical Data used by the Crime Prevention Support Unit

1. Spot mapping location of crime
     time of crime
     types of crime.

2. Information charts detailing
   (a) offences committed in crime areas
   (b) monthly analysis of specific crimes categorised by time and whether committed in crime areas.

3. Overall comparisons between crime areas and
   (a) Restaurants and cafes
   (b) Public transport and car parks
   (c) Educational establishments
   (d) Licensed premises.

4. Spot distribution maps displaying approximate location of home addresses of young people (under the age of seventeen years) who admitted a criminal offence(s).

5. Detailed analysis of 'juveniles at risk' areas categorised by age and main offence for which (s)he became known.

6. Detailed analysis of six categories of juvenile crime showing age trends.

7. Graphs identifying areas with 'increasing', 'constant' or 'decreasing' numbers of juvenile offenders.

8. In-depth analysis of 'increasing' areas.

9. Comparison of crime areas with areas of 'juveniles at risk'.

10. Areas of 'juveniles at risk' seen in relation to areas with
    (a) High proportion of children 0 – 14 years
    (b) High proportion of bus users
    (c) Council housing and multi-occupancy dwellings
    (d) Car ownership
    (e) Sports, pleasure and recreational grounds
    (f) High proportion of skilled and unskilled workers
    (g) High proportion of single-parent families and high social
        service case loads
    (h) Youth clubs and other youth amenities such as Scouts,
        Guides and 5-a-side football clubs.

Appendix C. Tables 1–11

Table 1a

STRENGTH OF SUPPORT FOR REACTIVE SUGGESTIONS	Agencies	Community	Resident Constables	City Centre Constables	Senior Officers
Police should have more powers to arrest	2.46	3.97	3.38	3.75	3.21
A mobile group of policemen should be available in a city to tackle delinquency	3.58	4.24	3.25	3.88	3.87
Police should concentrate more resources on catching young people who break the law	2.77	4.28	3.75	4.13	3.44
Strengthening the police by increasing their numbers would contain the delinquency problem	3.07	4.29	4.63	3.63	3.66
Overall	2.97	4.20	3.75	3.85	3.55
No. of Responses	17	21	8	8	16

Table 1b

STRENGTH OF SUPPORT FOR PREVENTIVE SUGGESTIONS	Agencies	Community	Resident Constables	City Centre Constables	Senior Officers
Policemen should help to set up or work with neighbourhood associations in tackling delinquency	4.60	4.80	4.50	3.62	4.58
Increasing the number of uniformed foot patrols would at least contain delinquency	3.94	4.44	4.50	4.00	4.13
Policemen should work in partnership with social workers, probation and others to tackle delinquency	4.71	4.29	4.37	3.37	4.58
Policemen should be encouraged to run discos and other activities for young people	3.70	3.86	3.12	2.50	3.84
Overall	4.24	4.35	4.12	3.37	4.28
No. of Responses	17	21	8	8	16

Table 2

	Agencies	Community	Resident Constables	City Centre Constables	Senior Officers
REACTIVE SUGGESTIONS					
Tougher punishments	–	7	8	30	4
Increased detection rate	–	7	8	8	13
Increased police powers	–	–	–	8	–
Increased police resources	–	–	–	8	8
PREVENTIVE SUGGESTIONS					
Preventive patrolling	37	26	31	8	22
Police/community involvement	26	53	7	30	36
Other agencies' social policies	–	7	31	8	4
Statutory agency/police partnership	37	–	15	–	13
	100%	100%	100%	100%	100%
No. of Responses*	16	15	13	13	23

* Multiple choice

Table 3

THE ORDER IN WHICH RESPONDENTS WOULD IMPLEMENT SPECIFIC POLICING PROPOSALS IN CRIME AREAS	Agencies	Community	Resident Constables	City Centre Constables	Senior Officers
1. Ask the magistrates to cut back the opening hours of night clubs.	6	4	6	6	1
2. Draft extra policemen into crime area from other parts of the town	4	6	1	1	3
3. Request late night transport in line with licensing hours	1	1	2	2	2
4. Arrange for plain clothes policemen to patrol area	5	1	2	5	6
5. Implement a crime prevention survey at all premises in area	2	3	4	4	3
6. Employ uniformed policemen on overtime to patrol 'high risk' crime areas during late evening/nights	2	5	5	2	5
No. of Responses	17	21	8	8	16

Table 4

RESPONDENTS OWN PROPOSALS FOR POLICING A CRIME AREA	Agencies	Community	Resident Constables	City Centre Constables	Senior Officers
REACTIVE SUGGESTIONS:					
Alcohol – strict police supervision and increased penalties	23	43	–	–	50
Aggressive patrolling	–	14	–	–	–
PREVENTIVE SUGGESTIONS:					
Environmental control	31	29	50	100	50
Community information	46	14	–	–	–
Preventive patrolling	–	–	50	–	–
	100%	100%	100%	100%	100%
No. of Responses*	13	7	2	2	4

*Multiple choice

Table 5

SHOULD POLICE INVOLVE THEMSELVES IN JUVENILE DELINQUENCY ABOVE AND BEYOND ARRESTING YOUNG PEOPLE?	Agencies	Community	Resident Constables	City Centre Constables	Senior Officers
Yes	100	85	75	62	100
No	–	5	25	38	–
Don't know	–	10	–	–	–
	100%	100%	100%	100%	100%
No. of Responses	17	21	8	8	16

Table 6

ORDER OF PRIORITY IN WHICH RESPONDENTS WOULD INTRODUCE POLICING OPTIONS IN AN AREA OF HIGH DELINQUENCY	Agencies	Community	Resident Constables	City Centre Constables	Senior Officers
1. Police to approach other statutory agencies such as social services, schools, youth and community, to set up action group to tackle problem	1	2	1	1	1
2. Police should approach the neighbourhood association and seek assistance in helping young people on the estate	2	1	2	3	2
3. Increase the numbers of police foot patrols on estate	3	3	3	2	3
4. Police should set up their own activity schemes i.e. weekend camps and football	4	3	5	6	4
5. Put a mobile group of uniform policemen into that neighbourhood	5	5	4	5	4
6. Increase arrests and prosecutions of young offenders	6	5	6	4	6
No. of Responses	17	21	8	8	16

Table 7

THE PERCENTAGE OF RESPONDENTS WHO THINK THAT THESE AGENCIES CAN HELP REMEDY THE PROBLEMS OF AREAS OF HIGH DELINQUENCY	Agencies	Community	Resident Constables	City Centre Constables	Senior Officers
Social services	100	52	87	62	86
Youth and community	100	86	100	87	94
Schools	94	76	100	75	78
Neighbourhood associations	88	81	100	62	94
Probation	82	38	87	37	82
Councillors	82	33	100	37	82
Housing	82	24	87	78	60
Transport	76	24	75	50	34
Planners	65	43	87	37	78
Health	59	10	37	25	29
Highways	53	14	50	12	40
ALSO SUGGESTED:					
Playgroups	42	–	–	–	–
Church	21	24	–	–	–
Young people	21	–	–	–	–
Press	–	–	–	12	34
General public	–	33	–	25	–
Uniformed organisations	–	–	–	25	–
Parents	–	33	–	–	–
No. of Responses	17	21	8	8	16

Table 8

WAYS IN WHICH AGENCIES AND ORGANISATIONS CAN ALLEVIATE PROBLEMS OF 'JUVENILES AT RISK' AREAS	Agencies	Community	Resident Constables	City Centre Constables	Senior Officers
By improving their decision making	30	42	40	29	29
By developing joint problem solving	42	34	49	34	42
By supplying amenities and/or services	28	24	11	37	29
	100%	100%	100%	100%	100%
No. of Responses*	105	131	60	40	70

*Multiple choice

Table 9

IS DATA ON 'JUVENILES AT RISK' AREAS OF USE TO YOU?	Agencies	Community	Police
Yes	100	82	88
No	–	9	9
Don't Know	–	9	3
	100%	100%	100%
No. of Responses	17	21	32

Table 10

HOW RESPONDENTS WOULD USE DATA ON 'JUVENILES AT RISK' AREAS	Agency	Community	Police
1. To take specific action within own organisation	33	50	20
2. To activate or seek co-operation of other agencies	19	29	43
3. To improve one's own understanding	48	21	37
	100%	100%	100%
No. of Responses	21	14	30

Table 11

HOW POLICEMEN WOULD USE DATA ON 'JUVENILES AT RISK' AREAS	Police
1. Planning and deployment of resources (without special objective)	33%
2. Preventive proposals	50%
3. Preventive and reactive proposals	10%
4. Reactive proposals	7%
	100%
No. of Responses	30